EXEMPLARS

Your Best Resource to Improve Student Writing

GRAHAM FOSTER

TONI L. MARASCO

Pembroke Publishers Limited

Pembroke Publishers
538 Hood Road
Markham, Ontario, Canada L3R 3K9
www.pembrokepublishers.com

Distributed in the U.S. by Stenhouse Publishers
480 Congress Street
Portland, ME 04101
www.stenhouse.com

We acknowledge the financial support of the Government of Canada through the Book
Publishing Industry Development Program (BPIDP) for our publishing activities.

We acknowledge the Government of Ontario through the Ontario Media Development
Corporation's Ontario Book Initiative.

Library and Archives Canada Cataloguing in Publication

Foster, Graham
    Exemplars : your best resource to improve student writing / Graham Foster and Toni
L. Marasco.

Includes index.
ISBN 978-1-55138-218-0

1. English language—Composition and exercises—Study and teaching (Elementary)
2. English language—Composition and exercises—Study and teaching (Secondary)
3. School prose, Canadian (English) I. Marasco, Toni L. II. Title.

LB1576.F6965 2007   372.62'3044   C2007-904158-2

Editor: Kate Revington
Cover Design: John Zehethofer
Typesetting: Jay Tee Graphics Ltd.

Printed and bound in Canada
9 8 7 6 5 4 3 2 1

Contents

Introduction: The Expanding Role of Exemplars 5

    Exemplars as an Instructional Resource 5
    Learning from Work with Exemplars 9
    Principles for Collecting Exemplars 12
    Developing Instructional Resources from Exemplars 13

1. Strategies 14

    Thinking About Strong Writing 15
    Identifying Specific Strategies 20
    Revising with Specific Criteria 22
    Focused Goal Setting 24
    How the Pros Do It 27
    Reconsidering Interpretations 30
    Effective Planning Strategies 33

2. Content 36

    Relevant and Irrelevant Detail—Informational Text 37
    Relevant and Irrelevant Detail—Narrative Text 39
    Writing Variables for Focus and Inspiration 41
    Engaging Story Beginnings and Endings 43
    Strong Endings for Narrative Texts 48
    Openings for Expository Texts 50
    Effective and Ineffective Topic Sentences 52
    Showing, Not Telling 55
    Titles That Work 57
    Playful Exemplar Activity — Off-Topic Sentence Insertions 59

3. Organization 61

    Pre-Writing for Business Letters 62
    Somebody, Wanted, But, So, Then 66
    Pre-Writing for Exposition 68
    Pre-Writing for Comparison and Contrast 70
    Paragraphing with Pizzazz 72
    Terrific Transition 74
    Text Sequencing to Learn About Transition 77
    Playful Exemplar Activities — Paragraph Play 80
    Planning a Myth 82

4. Sentence Variety *84*

    Complex Sentences *85*
    Sentence Combining for Interest and Clarity *88*
    Sentence Combining to Show Relationships *90*
    Varied Sentence Beginnings *92*
    Varied Sentence Types *94*
    The Power of Short Sentences *96*
    Playful Exemplar Activity — Simplifying the Complex *98*
    Sentence Structure and Word Choice *100*

5. Word Choice *103*

    Cloze for Colorful Vocabulary *104*
    Precise and Imprecise Word Choice *106*
    The Vocabulary Thing *109*
    Colorful Choices *111*
    Verb Challenge *113*
    Assessing Word Choice *115*
    To Be or Not to Be *117*
    Adding Rich Details *119*
    Choices in Context *122*
    Playful Exemplar Activity — From Descriptive to Dull *125*

6. Voice *127*

    Honest, Original Expression *128*
    Original Imagery *130*
    First-Person Writing and Dialogue *132*
    Intensifying Voice *134*
    Imaginative Detail and Use of Devices *138*

7. Conventions *140*

    Learning Parts of Speech *141*
    Standard Usage Mini-Lessons *144*
    Dictation Exercises to Learn Conventions *146*
    Editing Codes *148*

Appendixes:

    Self-Assessment of Writing *151*
    How the Pros Do It *152*
    Reconsidering Interpretations *153*
    Pre-Writing for Exposition *154*

Index *155*

    Acknowledgments *160*

Introduction: The Expanding Role of Exemplars

Over the past few years, many teachers have collected exemplars to set standards for writing. Typically, they employ exemplars as complements to rubrics with high, average, and low papers selected to demonstrate varied levels of achievement. Exemplars *show* what rubrics tell about assessment criteria. Usually referenced to grade levels, they illustrate student work in a way that may help other students improve their work. They need not be print samples. For instance, an exemplar may be a piece of student art or a videotape of a debate.

Exemplars as an Instructional Resource

While exemplars possess immense value in standard setting, wise teachers employ them as teaching tools, as well.

The next years will certainly mark increased use of exemplars, not only to establish standards for writing, but also to instruct. Just as the past 10 years saw a proliferation in the use of rubrics to assess student writing—witness the collection of rubrics in teachers' guides, on Web sites, and in bulletins related to large-scale writing assessments—teachers will become increasingly imaginative in planning student work using exemplars. Exemplars are so valuable as part of teachers' toolboxes that they should be employed regularly across grades and subjects. They are indispensable learning resources for students.

Many teachers already collect a variety of exemplars, including writing exemplars, to work with future groups of students. Through exemplars, teachers show rather than tell program expectations for learning tasks, including those for writing. For example, a Grade 6 teacher and a Grade 9 teacher may be instructing students about business letter writing. The language they use to describe effective business letters will probably be similar; however, Grade 6 and Grade 9 exemplars will show students not only desirable features of business letters, but the expected level of achievement in business letters for those grades.

In employing grade-level exemplars as instructional resources, teachers recognize that rubrics published for a grade level employ language that is repeated at other grade levels. For example, rubrics may call for "insightful content" in both Grade 5 and in Grade 9. What does "insightful content" mean for each grade? The higher grade will, of course, demand higher standards, but exemplars are required to illustrate the differences and to help students understand the expectations of a writing task at their learning level or grade.

The rubric on page 7 is based on six traits of good writing—content, organization, sentence variety, word choice, voice, and conventions. These six traits characterize effective writing in the following ways:

- *Content:* The content presented is appropriate and relevant to the author's purpose, and interesting, original details are included.
- *Organization:* The writing has a logical beginning, middle, and ending, with transitions helping the reader understand the connections between sections.
- *Sentence variety:* Variation in sentence type and length adds interest to the writing and shows the relationships between ideas. For example, to suggest speed and action, an author may employ a sequence of simple sentences—these would serve the author's purpose.
- *Word choice:* It should be precise and appropriate to purpose and audience. Consider that words with rich connotations are often effective in literary text, but not in scientific text.
- *Voice:* Writing characterized by voice demonstrates that the writer cares about the content and presents an honest, personal perspective about the topic. A writer's voice is expressed through originality in detail and word choice—the greatest enemy of voice is the cliché.
- *Conventions:* Usually, effective writing employs conventional spelling, punctuation, and usage; however, the language can be purposefully and effectively unconventional when an author presents the unique dialect of a region or group.

The language in the rubric is typical of rubrics currently used by teachers and students in different grades.

Although rubrics usefully instruct students about expectations for writing, they are much more powerful when used with exemplars. How can exemplars be optimally employed so that students will improve their writing skills? This book illustrates possibilities for engaging instruction that draws on exemplars as a writing resource. Students can employ exemplars to learn about the content, organization, sentence structure, word choice, voice, and conventions of effective writing. Since exemplars can also help them learn about writing strategies, the first activities in this resource offer practical suggestions in that regard. The carefully chosen exemplars featured span Grades 4 to 9; since they are intended to represent exemplars generally—and teachers typically encounter a wide range of ability in their classrooms—these exemplars are not labelled by grade.

Exemplars can enable students to think about an author's choices. The more than 50 activities in this book challenge students to think about a writer's options and to transfer what they learn to their own writing. Although using exemplars without students revising work in response may have some value, in general, students benefit most when they apply what they have just been taught.

This book, with its exemplar-based mini-lessons, allows teachers to take a flexible and natural approach to addressing specific student writing needs. Teachers can readily use exemplars to differentiate instruction within a class. Choice of lesson topic is best made on identified student need. If teachers observe that some students lack sentence variety in their writing, for example, they could use related exemplars as teaching tools to address that need. After a mini-lesson, the students could then revise some of their own work with that trait in mind.

	Content	Organization	Sentence Variety	Word Choice	Voice	Conventions
5	Writing consistently captivates readers' interest. Writing consistently contains original content. Writer's purpose is clearly evident. Writing focus is clearly maintained.	Beginnings and endings command attention. Ideas are consistently presented in a clear order. Transitions are consistently employed effectively.	Sentence type and complexity are consistently controlled and varied.	Words are consistently appropriate, effective, and purposefully selected.	Writing consistently employs unique content, imagery, and vocabulary. Writing consistently demonstrates caring and honesty.	Usage, spelling, and punctuation are consistently correct.
4	Writing has original content. Writing often captivates reader's interest. Writing purpose is usually evident. Writing focus is usually maintained.	Beginnings and endings provide direction. Ideas are usually presented in a clear order. Transitions are usually employed effectively.	Sentence type and complexity are usually controlled and varied.	Words are usually appropriate, effective, and purposefully selected.	Writing usually employs unique content, imagery, and vocabulary. Writing usually demonstrates caring and honesty.	Usage, spelling, and punctuation are usually correct.
3	Writing generally holds the readers' interest. Writing contains predictable content. Writer's purpose is generally evident. Writing focus is maintained.	Beginnings and endings are predictable. Ideas are generally presented in a clear order. Transitions are sometimes employed.	Sentence type and complexity are sometimes controlled and varied.	Words are sometimes appropriate, effective, and purposefully selected.	Writing sometimes employs unique content, imagery, and vocabulary. Writing sometimes demonstrates caring and honesty.	Usage, spelling, and punctuation are sometimes correct.
2	Writing does not hold the readers' interest. Writing contains some irrelevant content. The writer's purpose is not always evident.	Beginnings and endings are sometimes confusing. Ideas are seldom presented in a clear order. Transitions are seldom employed.	Sentences illustrate limited variety in type and complexity.	Words are often imprecise and redundant.	Writing rarely employs unique content, imagery, and vocabulary. Writing rarely demonstrates caring and honesty.	Usage, spelling, and punctuation are inconsistently correct.
1	Writing is confusing for the reader. Writing lacks relevant content. The writer's purpose is not evident. Writing lacks focus.	Beginnings and endings are unclear or lacking. Content lacks clear order. Transitions are not employed.	Sentences illustrate no variation in type and complexity.	Words are often unclear, misused, and inaccurate.	Writing does not include unique content, imagery, and vocabulary. Writing does not demonstrate caring and honesty.	Usage, spelling, and punctuation are so incorrect as to impede meaning.

Activities in this book can be appropriately employed for a range of groupings. When large numbers of students would benefit from focused instruction, teachers will conduct whole-class lessons. When some students demonstrate a common need in their writing, teachers will work with small groups. After a student–teacher conference, teachers could direct individual students to complete an activity.

Some experts in writing assessment suggest that, in responding to student writing, teachers should note one positive feature and offer one or two key suggestions; if teachers offer many suggestions, they draw attention to none.

A range of learning activities appears in this resource. More than 25 activities challenge students to work with a single exemplar or brief exemplar set. Nine activities challenge students to choose between pieces of writing completed by two different students. Six activities challenge students to choose the preferred version of two texts written by one student. One activity challenges students to assess the student's original and an enhanced version of the text.

For 10 activities, students work with two versions of an exemplar: the student writer's original text and a modified or degraded version. In instances such as these, a few key words may be blacked out, two complex sentences rewritten as simple sentences, or the concluding sentence replaced with a blank line. The learning activity might be to insert precise and connotative words for those blacked out, to combine the simple sentences into an effective complex sentence, or to compose an effective concluding sentence. Students then examine the original version of the exemplar to compare their choices with those made by the student author of the exemplar. To their amazement, students often discover that their choices work as effectively, if not more effectively than choices made by the author of the exemplar.

The following chart illustrates a typical learning sequence:

Learning Sequence for Work with Writing Exemplars

1. Students and teachers build background on the instructional focus for work with exemplars. For instance, if the lesson focus is on complex sentences, teachers engage students in a mini-lesson on complex sentences and ways to add complexity to sentences.

2. Students receive a modified version of the exemplar, such as an exemplar with blacked-out words or lines or clearly marked changes to the original text. Modified versions focus on specific writing features, such as word choice, sentence structure, transition, endings, or matters of usage.

   OR

   Students receive two versions of an exemplar: the original version and a modified version with clearly marked points for comparison.

3. Students consider options for the modified text related to specific instruction.

   OR

   Students assess which of the two versions of the exemplar demonstrates superior performance with points marked for comparison.

4. Students revise a piece of their own writing, applying specific criteria related to their work with exemplars. By so doing, they can transfer what they learned from working with exemplars to their own writing, making it better.

The approach outlined in step 4 is consistent with research reported by George Hillocks in *Research on Written Composition: New Directions for Teaching* (National Council Teachers of English 1986):

> Students who have been actively involved in the use of specific criteria and/or questions to judge texts of their own or others, write compositions of significantly higher quality than those who have not. (p. 24)

> As a group these studies conclude rather clearly that engaging young writers actively in the use of criteria, applied to their own and each others' writing, results not only in more effective revisions but in superior first drafts. (p. 160)

Research clearly establishes that students internalize qualities of effective writing when they apply specific criteria to their own writing. Therefore, students should attend to specific features in their own writing as they learn about targeted skills through exemplars.

Some teachers will note a similarity in this suggested instructional sequence with the long-established Prose Models approach. Instead of working with exemplars of students' writing, you could employ the work of professional authors. Writing by published authors has been featured in textbooks and writing handbooks for generations. However, teachers who have employed student exemplars to complement adult writing samples report a significant motivational benefit for students.

Remember that the exemplar typically represents the writing of a student at that grade level. Most students recognize that they will not write as well as professional writers; however, they often recognize that they *can* match or exceed the writing of the grade-level exemplar. This motivational benefit has been reported by teachers across grades and subjects:

- After her class's work with exemplars, a Grade 3 teacher heard a student say this about story writing: "I can do even better than that in my own story."
- A junior high teacher who has collected exemplars of expository essays for several years notes that the quality of student writing improves over time. Students report that they can exceed the quality of exemplars collected, displayed, and studied in the classroom.
- A Grade 5 teacher recognized benefits to assessment from use of exemplars. After work with exemplars, students in her class noted that they couldn't complain about their marks: the exemplars clearly showed them the expectations for the assignment.

Exemplars featured in this book have been collected by teachers who regularly employ exemplars as an instructional resource. These teachers recognize that exemplars are more powerful in instruction than alternative learning resources, such as texts about writing without writing samples or samples selected only from the work of professional writers.

Learning from Work with Exemplars

Students, too, note how exemplars benefit their learning how to write effectively.
After work with exemplars to improve word choice, a teacher asked her Grade

4 class to respond in writing to this question: "How can looking at writing samples improve your writing?" Student responses included these:

- It helps me improve because if they have perfect writing then you can learn from them.
- I can improve my writing by using more descriptive words to give the reader a picture of what is happening.
- It helps because you can see theirs and see how they did it.
- You can learn things to compare to your story and make sure it is more descriptive and interesting.
- Because I can see examples of stuff to change.

The class worked with the exemplars "Mysterious Box" (page 89) and "A Trip to the Future" (page 120). As a class, students suggested improved word choice for "Mysterious Box," including these:

I <u>walked</u> over to the big box.
(charged, ran, trudged, bolted)
Unfortunately, it was too dark to <u>take a look.</u>
(sneak a look, notice what was inside)

After full-class work, the teacher provided each student with four small sticky notes and challenged students to scan a current piece of writing, underline words that could beneficially be changed, and mark more effective word choices on sticky notes placed above underlined words.

These revisions demonstrate benefits evident in most students' work:

Student one:
- *Original:* The bear <u>stood </u>on its hind legs.
  Revised: The bear <u>rose up</u> on its hind legs.
- *Original:* A small fawn galloped in front of it and <u>took off</u>.
  Revised: A small fawn galloped in front of it and <u>scurried off</u>.

Student two:
- *Original:* My best friend Sam and I were <u>walking</u> home.
  Revised: My best friend Sam and I were <u>trudging</u> home.
- *Original:* l <u>walked</u> into the room.
  Revised: I <u>tiptoed</u> into the room.

Student three:
- *Original:* I <u>moved</u> on.
  Revised: I <u>charged</u> on.
- *Original:* I opened the door and <u>looked</u> on the bed.
  Revised: I opened the door and <u>peered</u> on the bed.

Although teachers may prefer other word choices to these, the revisions do show evidence of incremental gains, which is what they are most likely to see.

In another documented instance of working with exemplars, a teacher decided to help Grade 6 students improve the endings in their writing. She worked with the exemplars "Confidential Key" (page 76) and "A Profession Without Equal" (page 81). Interestingly, both of these exemplars appear in this resource for reasons other than work with endings—many exemplars can be employed for instructional objectives beyond those featured here.

After discussion of the two exemplars and of the endings of a few published informational and narrative texts, students generated the following list of possibilities for endings:

- summarizing (informational text)
- emphasizing a final point (informational text)
- moralizing (fables)
- presenting a surprising twist (narratives)
- showing a changed attitude (narratives)
- presenting the central character's reaction (narratives)

Individual students then used sticky notes to revise an ending to a piece of writing—or to comment on why their current ending was effective.

These revisions demonstrate benefits evident in most students' work:

Student one:
- *Original:* Finally, scuba diving on the coast was the highlight of my trip.
  Revised: While the scuba diving on the coast was the highlight of my trip, I realized that I have only begun my travel adventures.

Student two:
- *Original:* Next is the food court. There are also plenty of fast food restaurants. The food fills me up no matter what. Some can be junk food and some can be healthy for you. The food court is a nutritious or not so good place for some.
  Revised: West Edmonton Mall offers enjoyable entertainment at the wave pool, the shops and the food court. I love the mall. For me, West Edmonton Mall is the best place to be!

Student three:
- *Original:* My new friend dashed away in the midway. My family was happy to see me safe. I liked my trip to the amusement park but I am extremely glad that I got home safely.
  Revised: My new friend dashed into the midway as my frantic parents hugged me. I made a new friend but it was not much of a friendship. Still, I wonder what happened to my friend.

At the conclusion of the activity, the teacher asked students to submit written responses to the question "How can looking at another student's writing and published writing help you improve your own writing?" Student responses included these:

- It helps because you can see better writing and improve your writing.
- I can learn where to place punctuation and add some jazz.
- Looking at other peoples' work helps me improve my writing because I can learn some words that I can use in my writing. It also would help me by teaching me how to end my story better.
- It helps because maybe you can learn something you didn't know how to do.

Some principles for collecting exemplars to help your students learn how to do something they may not have been able to do before are outlined next.

Principles for Collecting Exemplars

Look for exemplars that have instructional potential related to the rubric in use and to the six traits. Exemplars that represent exceptional grade-level work as well as those that represent less than perfect work have instructional potential. Exemplars of both types appear in this book.

Keep in mind, too, that an exemplar may model several desirable features in writing, such as effective transitions, word choices, and unique voice. Teachers may use a single exemplar to develop instructional material related to any of these traits. They may also choose to develop instructional material that is multi-focused. For example, one exemplar could be used for instruction in transitions, word choices, and voice. Multi-focused instructional materials with exemplars, such as the activity "Sentence Structure and Word Choice," are included in this book.

When collecting exemplars, be careful to respect privacy laws as well as school district guidelines. In collecting student work for use with other classes in subsequent years, be sure to remember these critical principles:

- Always present the exemplars anonymously.
- Always request permission from the student author and the student's parent/guardian.

Consider modifying the following letter and permission slip so that the documents more clearly reflect the privacy laws and school district guidelines that apply to your work:

Dear _____ :

I would very much like to employ the enclosed piece of writing by your child as an instructional resource with other classes. Such samples are useful in instructing students about important program expectations.

As is consistent with School District expectations, I am seeking approval for use of one of your child's pieces of work as a learning resource. If you are agreeable to this use, please sign the attached permission form.

I have already received your child's permission to use the work sample to help other students learn. Please be assured that your child's work will be presented anonymously and that it will always be honored as an instructional resource.

If you have any questions or concerns, please call me at _____.

Permission Form

Date _____

I grant permission for _____ School to employ the work of my child, _____, as an instructional resource, to be presented anonymously. The work is entitled "_____."

_____

Signature of Parent/Guardian

Developing Instructional Resources from Exemplars

The writers hope that this book will prompt teachers to develop their *own* instructional resources from exemplars of student writing.

This book offers instructional material that illustrates several possibilities:

- presenting an exemplar focused on a specific writing trait
- presenting two versions of a piece of writing completed by the same student
- presenting two versions of a piece of writing to instruct a targeted writing trait: one, the student writer's original text; the other, a degraded version of the text
- presenting two versions of a piece of writing: one, the student writer's original text; the other, an enhanced version of the text
- presenting two or three writing samples completed by different students to challenge students to choose the superior version

When teachers note instructional potential related to the traits of effective writing, reflected in rubrics, they gather exemplars—gathering becomes an ongoing practice. They use the exemplars to develop learning activities similar to those illustrated in this book. Typically over a school year, teachers meet to share exemplars and work together to develop imaginative and appropriate activities. Priorities for development of instructional material with exemplars will be determined by the needs of the class.

In discussion, teachers consider the instructional potential of each exemplar. As illustrated in this book, an exemplar can often be used to instruct in several traits of effective writing as well as strategies used by writers. Discussion will likely reveal instructional possibilities missed by the teacher working in isolation. Teachers need not be at the same grade level to brainstorm instructional possibilities for exemplars collected by individuals in their group. As noted earlier, a single exemplar may be employed for several different learning activities. Teachers should develop activities related to all key traits in the rubric.

Developing instructional resources becomes especially satisfying when completed with colleagues as a professional development activity—some of the instructional material in the following pages was developed by teachers who worked with colleagues to refine and share their work with exemplars.

Exemplars demonstrate expectations about writing to students; however, they can do much more. Well thought-out lessons with exemplars challenge students to think about a writer's choices, to judge effective and less effective choices. Effective lessons with exemplars respond to priorities evident in the students' own writing. When instruction with exemplars culminates with students revising pieces of their own writing, lessons with exemplars become even more powerful.

1. Strategies

Learning activities in this book feature exemplars to challenge students to improve important writing skills related to content, organization, sentence structure, word choice, voice, and conventional usage. Skills refer to *what* teachers expect students to demonstrate in their writing, for example, content appropriate to purpose and audience, controlled and varied sentences, and precise word choice.

This Strategies section helps students learn the importance of writing techniques used by writers to make their writing more effective. The message to students is that their improved ability to describe how they will complete a writing task improves the skillfulness of their compositions.

- **Thinking About Strong Writing** emphasizes that improving one's writing depends upon an understanding of what effective writing is and what language is used to describe effective writing.
- **Identifying Specific Strategies** reminds students of the value to writers of specific strategies that they will use before, during, and after writing the first draft.
- **Revising with Specific Criteria** explains how sticky notes help students mark specific revisions.
- **Focused Goal Setting** underlines the value of specific goal setting.
- **How the Pros Do It** demonstrates the strategy of using published texts to answer questions about one's writing.
- **Reconsidering Interpretations** illustrates the value of writing to refine one's interpretation of a text.
- **Effective Planning Strategies** stresses the value of individual students discovering approaches that work best for them before, during, and after writing their first draft.

Thinking About Strong Writing

Before working with exemplars related to a specific element or trait of writing, such as sentence structure or voice, teachers may choose to help students develop an understanding of language used to describe writing. Exemplars, such as the two featured at the end of this activity, are useful resources to help students learn about this language which they can then apply to their writing.

Begin by challenging the class to answer the question "What is good writing?" On chart paper, chalkboard, or whiteboard, record student responses. Probe by having students think of books or stories they consider to be well written. Depending on the grade and age of the students, responses might include the following:

- Good writing is exciting—it's interesting.
- The author uses good words.
- There are no spelling mistakes.
- The title makes you interested in reading.
- The writing has a clear beginning, middle, and end.
- Sentences are of different lengths.
- The punctuation seems correct.
- The writer really cares about the writing.
- It is easy to read.

Use student responses to help students learn about language used to describe writing. Classify student responses using this terminology:

- content—the ideas or events described
- organization—the way ideas are put in order and connected
- sentence structure—variety of sentence beginnings and lengths
- word choice—the effective use of words
- voice—the writer's unique way of writing
- conventions—spelling, punctuation, grammar and usage, and legibility

Most activities featured in this resource are identified and clustered by these terms, or key traits, of writing.

From here, you might want to engage students in discussion about the importance of purpose and audience. Writers make decisions about content, organization, sentence structure, word choice, voice, and conventions according to what they are trying to achieve—what their purpose is—and what they think will appeal to their audience. Sometimes, writers will break the rules of conventional usage to capture how people in a certain region or group speak. Sometimes, they use a series of short sentences to suggest quick action. Therefore, while the ideas about what constitutes good writing often apply, they do not always apply—the success of books by such award-winning, appealing authors as Jerry Spinelli attests to this. How we describe good writing relates to the writer's purpose and audience.

To have students think further about what makes strong writing, have them work alone or in groups to read the exemplars "Hockey Future" and "Smarty Pants and the Biggest Discovery" and decide whether the writing is strong, average, or weak. They must also give reasons for their assessments. In the sharing of responses, emphasize the terminology to describe writing. Once student responses are listed on the board or on an overhead, challenge students to classify the responses based on how closely they relate to content, organization, sentence structure, word choice, voice, and conventions. Work with students to label the responses accordingly. If students lack descriptors related to one or more of the traits, challenge them to identify an appropriate description.

Students may justify assessments that "Hockey Future" is an average or a weak composition. Possible reasons include the following:

Average	Weak
exciting action in plot (content)	lack of detail (content)
interesting title (content)	simple sentence patterns (sentence structure)
interesting detail about gadgets (content)	lack of color in word choice (word choice)
honest voice—The writer loves hockey! (voice)	weak ending (content)
uppercase text features for emphasis (conventions)	

Students may justify assessments of "Smarty Pants and the Biggest Discovery" as strong for reasons such as these:

- engaging dialogue (content)
- interesting title (content)
- descriptive language (word choice)
- strong opener (content)
- strong ending (content)
- easy to follow—effective transitions (organization)

Challenge students to refer to the text and to select examples to support their judgments. For example, the student who made the point about engaging dialogue might say: "The monkey's direct speech really punched out the ideas. The lines were really funny." On the other hand, areas for improvement include

- familiarity or lack of originality in content (content)
- run-on sentences (conventions)
- unclear meaning in places (content)
- paragraphing—the need to change paragraphs when speakers change (organization)

After they complete the work with exemplars, have students write specific assessments of the content, organization, sentence structure, word choice, voice, and conventions of one of their own compositions. Working alone or with a partner, students could complete a chart set up much like the following:

Self-Assessment of Writing		
Title of Composition: _____		
	Strengths	**Areas for Improvement**
Content		
Organization		
Sentence Structure		
Word Choice		
Voice		
Conventions		

This chart appears as a reproducible page on page 151.

Remind students that their writing will improve when they set goals (areas for improvement) and revise their writing with specific goals in mind. Challenge students to work with a partner to make one helpful change based on improvements identified on the chart. The change should be clearly marked on the composition, possibly with a sticky note. Sometimes, students will assess their writing inaccurately, applying criteria for revision inappropriately. When this happens, a genuine teachable moment is created. Teachers may helpfully focus students on effectively applying a criterion through a mini-lesson.

It is a good idea for students to complete more charts to assess compositions on their own or with a partner throughout the school year. The exercise should help students recognize their goals as learners and appreciate how exemplar activities, such as those in this book, will help them improve their writing. For instance, a student whose vocabulary is imprecise should identify "precise word choice" as an area for improvement; a student whose writing lacks needed paragraph structure should identify "effective paragraphing" as an area for improvement. Conferences with their teacher will confirm that students are accurate in their self-assessments. Since specific learning activities are best selected in response to needs demonstrated in students' writing, the student working on precise vocabulary could do an exemplar activity focused on word choice and the student working on improved paragraphing could complete an activity focused on organization.

Remind students that their work with exemplars will help them learn more about the language that describes writing. More important, students will use this language to think about writing choices to improve their own writing.

EXEMPLAR A

Hockey Future

One day there was a boy who loved hockey. He played all the time but one day he went to the future and saw what hockey was like in the year 3003. The skates had rockets on them, the net was smaller. The puck had magnets and the sticks had gadgets. I was walking when I saw the hockey rink. I went in and joined a Team. I had practice which I got used to the gadgets and puck. It was time for the game. I scored lots and distracted by using gadgets. I scored lots because I used the net magnet on the puck. The score was 12 – 0 for us with 5 seconds left in the game. I was coming up to the net. I pulled out a water gun from the stick, shot at the goalie and scored. "BUZZZZZZZZZZ!" went the Buzzer. We won. I said good bye to my teammates and went back to the present. That night I went to bed excited about my next future Adventure.

I think this piece of writing is _____ strong _____ average _____ weak because

1. _____

2. _____

3. _____

4. _____

5. _____

EXEMPLAR B

Smarty-Pants and the Biggest Discovery

Smarty-Pants the monkey had been born and raised in the New York Zoo. This particular zoo had the most talented animals in the world! These animals could read, write, and paint and talk! This Zoo was owned by Mr. and Mrs. Upjohn. Smarty-Pants loved the zoo, but he knew there was something beyond it. And he was determined to find it. Mr. and Mrs. Upjohn had two children, Tommy and Lilly and they were put in charge of the Zoo for a week, while their mom and dad were away. Smarty-Pants received the news from Elly Elephant, who got it from Dolly Dolphin who overheard Tommy and Lilly talking. "This is my chance!" thought Smarty-Pants. So he began to prepare! Instead of eating his dry food he saved it in his hay stack, he began to weave a bag out of straw, and make Elly give him some peanuts along with a peanut bag she had found; now he was ready. Two days later, in the afternoon, he coaxed Tommy and Lilly to leave the door open after they fed him. So after lots of encouragement they did. Smarty-Pants told the other animals his plan and they agreed that they would do the job Smarty-Pants gave them:

Leo Lion would lock them in his cage and Dolly would give them drinks of water and Elly would give them showers. Zoe Zebra would get the peanut bag and feed them peanuts.

Now Smarty would set off.

Smarty gave Zoe the peanut bag and headed out of the zoo, he crossed the road. Cars beeped, ladies screamed, men yelled. Smarty-Pants was terrified so he climbed a telephone pole and treated them like vines. He monkey-boned down the countryside, towns and cities. After two days he rested and had a snack of water, peanuts and dry food, then he set off again. While he was traveling he passed a sign that said, "Welcome to Florida!" Smarty-Pants froze, then he began thinking. Why am I here? What am I doing? He turned around had a snack and zipped back down the telephone poles. He didn't stop to mind beeps, screams, yells and barks till he was right back where he started. The animals all wanted to know what happened, but instead he asked them "Which one of my ridiculous ideas was this? "The craziest one," answered Elly. Then Smarty-Pants promised that he would never come to one of those ideas again. And he never did.

I think this piece of writing is _____ strong _____ average _____ weak because

1. _____

2. _____

3. _____

4. _____

5. _____

Identifying Specific Strategies

Exemplars can be used to help students identify personally effective writing strategies. The following page illustrates how two students describe strategies used before, during, and after their writing of a newspaper article as well as a primary goal for future writing.

With students working with a partner or in a small group, have them identify the superior of two exemplars and then describe why Exemplar A is superior in each of the four categories:

1. *Strategies Before Drafting*—Exemplar A identifies a specific strategy related to a type of writing—RAFTS (Role, Audience, Format, Topic, Strong verb, which is explained in detail on page 41); Exemplar B is too general to be very helpful.
2. *Strategies During Drafting*—Remind students to keep the flow going during drafting and to check writing later. The student who wrote Exemplar B would be wiser to focus on spell checks and neatness later. The student in Exemplar A realizes that the introduction is often the most challenging part of a composition and that her writing will flow if she writes the introduction last.
3. *Strategies After Drafting*—Research strongly argues for revision with specific rather than general criteria. Exemplar A demonstrates a specific focus; Exemplar B does not.
4. *Goal Setting*—Goals need to be specific to be implemented thoughtfully. Exemplar A illustrates specificity; Exemplar B does not.

In using these exemplars, emphasize to students that their writing will benefit if they can identify specific strategies for pre-writing, during-writing, and post-writing as well as goals. Obviously, students should identify different writing strategies for different tasks.

After their work with the exemplars, students should note strategies that they employ to complete writing tasks (see a possible framework below). Stress to them that they should be as specific as possible and that their thoughtful choices of strategies will improve their writing.

Topic_____

Name _____ Date _____

Identifying Strategies

Strategies Before Drafting

Strategies During Drafting

Strategies After Drafting

Goal Setting

Understanding Myself as a Writer

Title of Text: Our School Trip to Newfoundland

Format: Newspaper article

Exemplar A	Exemplar B
Strategies That I Used Before Drafting I used a thought web and RAFTS.	**Strategies That I Used Before Drafting** I always brainstorm before writing.
Strategies That I Used During Drafting I began with the second paragraph and wrote my introduction last. I wrote on every second line.	**Strategies That I Used During Drafting** I checked on correct spelling as I wrote. I kept my writing neat.
Strategies That I Used After Drafting I checked spelling. I replaced dull words with descriptive words. I changed parts that were not clear.	**Strategies That I Used After Drafting** I read it over to make it better.
My Writing Goal I want to improve the introductions of my next story.	**My Writing Goal** I want to make my writing more interesting.

Revising with Specific Criteria

Research strongly argues for revising one's writing with specific criteria. Writers internalize important writing features when they check their own work for specific writing features, such as colorful vocabulary, varied sentences, clarity of detail, and effective transitions—editing with specific criteria is equally valuable.

The following exemplar illustrates how sticky notes can be employed as an effective means for students to revise with specific criteria. In consultation with their teacher, students wrote a selected criterion on each sticky note, attached the sticky notes to their pages, and drew in pencil to indicate that their writing effectively illustrated each criterion.

The students and their teacher agreed to focus on the following criteria:

- at least two precise words
- showing, not telling (see activity "Showing, Not Telling," on pages 55–56)
- a sentence that begins with something other than the subject
- an effective introduction technique, such as suspenseful detail, dialogue that illustrates a conflict, a dramatic event, or a setting that highlights movement or action related to the story's conflict
- meeting of a personal writing goal

In working with each criterion, students often discover that their writing does not illustrate at least one desirable trait. In that case, they must revise their text so that they can mark the illustration of each criterion.

Note that in the exemplar illustration, the student chose "correct use of the apostrophe" as her personal goal. However, her use of the apostrophe is incorrect since for plural possession, she should have written *parents'* rather than *parent's*. The student will review the rule for use of the apostrophe and will use the criterion on the next composition to illustrate correct use of the apostrophe.

Use the exemplar to illustrate the sticky note method for revision with specific criteria. You can either show it on an overhead projector or supply each student with a photocopy of the page. Then, in consultation with you, students can note appropriate specific criteria on about five sticky notes and use pencil lines to indicate that their own writing effectively illustrates each criterion.

EXEMPLAR

Disappointment

Correct use of the apostrophe — my personal goal

Joan was walking in front of her parent's summer home collecting seashells. She had collected about everything that had caught her eye, when, while walking back, she stumbled upon an old rusty bottle. It seemed to have something in it so she went for a closer look.

Introduction created interest through suspense

My most precise words

She had been right in her judging—there was a note inside. She took the bottle home, cracked it open and immediately began reading:

> "To whoever finds this, my name is Judy.
> I'm 13 and looking for a pen-pal."

The note went on listing hobbies, favorite things, grade and other things describing her. Most of the note had been rubbed out, but that didn't stop Joan; she pulled out a piece of paper and began writing. She then sent it to the address indicated. Now all she had to do was wait.

The letter had been a long awaited item, and when it arrived it was received with enthusiasm and open arms. It read:

> "Dear Joan,
> It was very nice of you to write back,
> but I am sorry to say that I wrote that note at least
> 17 years ago. I'm sorry if I disappointed you.
>   Judy"

My best showing not telling.

A saddened look came over Joan's face. She was disappointed, upset, and angry most of all. She sat down and began writing down her name, address and other information. Then, taking one of her father's wine bottles, she stuck the note inside. She then walked out to the beach and threw the bottle as far as she could and hoped that someone would go through the same things.

A sentence that begins with something other than the subject

The year was 2003 A.D. Chris was swimming in the intergalactic sea pit when she felt something under her foot. It was an antique-looking wine bottle......

Focused Goal Setting

Students improve their writing when they regularly set personal goals and when they note achievement of the goals. Throughout the school year, have students keep a goals chart similar to the one printed below. The chart encourages students to identify personal learning challenges and to celebrate achievement of learning outcomes.

My Personal Writing Goals

Goals	Goals Achieved

The following exemplars illustrate the value of goal-setting activities. At set times throughout the school year, probably at the completion of major writing tasks, have students make notations about their goals and goals achieved, perhaps on a framework such as the chart below.

Exemplar B represents improved writing related to student goal setting. The student writer completed goal setting as follows:

My Personal Writing Goals

Goals	Goals Achieved
• Add original figures of speech and comparisons (October 15)	• Revised "A Fish Story" with original figures of speech (November 3)

A Fish Story

Grampa is always telling me stories. Once he said that the snowflakes in his day were just huge. He said that he caught a fish twice the size of a regular fish. This story is my favorite.....

"Well, my boy, do you want to hear a story?" Grampa would always say. "It's about how my trip to school was every day of the year."

"I don't see why not," I would say, even though I had heard this story many times.

"Well … First I had to climb a huge mountain. Through blizzards so bad they knocked down trees. I dodged and swerved around the falling trees. When I got to the top of the mountain, there was a waterfall. The waterfall was super long. I took a boat down it. Giant waves splashed and crashed. There were fish in the water that were huge! They had really big teeth, and fins like you couldn't believe! At the end of my boat ride I had to walk a zillion miles. And then finally after this long adventure, I just made it to school in time for the end of school bell to ring. Boy was the teacher mad."

A Fish Story

Grampa is always telling me interesting yarns. Once he said that the snowflakes in his day were like fluffy white elephants. He said that he caught a fish darn near twice the size of his head. But this story has always been my favorite……..

"Well, my dear boy, do you want to hear a story," Grampa would always begin, "of what my trip to school every day entailed?"

"I don't see why not," I would say, even though I had heard this story a thousand times.

"Well … First I had to climb up a mountain as tall as a ten story building. Through blizzards so strong that whole forests would fall in their wake. I dodged and swerved around the toppling trees. When I reached the summit of the mountain, there was a waterfall. The waterfall was as long as the Great Wall of China. I had to take a rickety old scow down it. Killer waves splashed and crashed. There were fish in the water that were monsters! They had fangs like a dinosaur, and fins like you wouldn't believe! At the end of my boat ride I had to walk 800 miles. Finally, after this long adventure, I just made it to school in time for the end of school bell to ring. And for some bizarre reason, the teacher wouldn't believe this was why I was late."

November 3 revision

How the Pros Do It

The following exemplars represent student work in a class completing a How the Pros Do It activity. The goal is to have students use published writing to learn specific techniques for their own writing. Students complete the following learning sequence.

1. Students note a question about their own writing: in the following exemplars, two students ask about making the beginnings of their stories interesting for the reader.
2. Students are challenged to review a set number of texts that they have recently read to note how published authors deal with the question. In the example of questioning how authors add interest to the beginnings of their stories, students would note techniques such as
   - presenting a dialogue related to conflict
   - plunging the reader into a conflict or dramatic event
   - introducing suspense or making the reader wonder about something
   - describing a setting with a focus on movement or action related to the story's conflict

3. Students decide how the answers to their question can be applied to their own writing.

Exemplar A illustrates that the student did not understand that he should look for *specific* answers to questions. It is very typical in that many students ask questions that are so general they are not helpful—many students have trouble with this activity, although older students tend to do better. Often, students benefit from working with a partner or in a small group to complete the activity. Follow-up class discussion would consider the value of specific learning inferred from professional writers. If you find that your students are struggling, though, you will have to decide whether the activity is promising enough to try again and again.

Exemplar B, on the other hand, illustrates specificity. By challenging students to choose the better work, teachers emphasize the value of specific information employed to answer questions to improve writing.

After their work with exemplars, prompt students to develop their own "How the Pros Do It" pages or provide copies of the reproducible sheet in the Appendixes. They will seek specific answers to questions they pose about their writing.

How the Pros Do It

I have this question about my own writing: *How can I make my introduction more interesting?*	

Below I have listed two or three texts that may help me answer my question.	Below I have written how the texts answer my questions; there may also be an excerpt that helps me answer my question.
"One Proud Summer" by Martha Hewitt *"The Only Wheelchair in Town" by Rick Hansen and Jim Taylor*	*I followed the steps by asking about introductions. I chose two stories. The stories helped me answer my questions by teaching me to do research.*

How the Pros Do It

I have this question about my own writing:

How can I make my introduction more interesting?

Below I have listed two or three texts that may help me answer my question.	Below I have written how the texts answer my questions; there may also be an excerpt that helps me answer my question.
"Waiting" by Budge Wilson *"The Smallest Dragonboy" by Anne McCaffrey*	*"You must realize, of course, that Julliette is a very complex child." My mother was talking on the telephone. Shouting, to be more exact."* *- I wondered why Juliette is complex and why the mother is shouting.* *"Although Kevan lengthened his walking stride as far as his legs would stretch, he couldn't quite keep up with the other candidates. He knew he would be teased again."* *- The author shows the main character's conflict—dealing with being smaller than other boys and dealing with being teased.*

Reconsidering Interpretations

Although this section will appear to relate more to reading than to writing, students frequently employ writing as a strategy to develop and demonstrate their understanding of text, often a literary text. The following exemplars, which show how students have checked their understanding of texts at different times, should help students learn about the value of their own writing to refine their interpretations of another text.

While exemplar pairs in this book often present a preferred option and an interior option, in this case, the exemplars illustrate two acceptable responses.

Challenge students to examine the exemplars to assess

- the value of checking text to confirm interpretation—how has checking text enhanced understanding?
- the value of discussing the text with others—how has discussion with others enhanced understanding?

Often, readers settle on meaning too quickly. Especially when they are answering questions, students should check the text before they respond. As the second bulleted point suggests, students benefit from a reminder that readers enhance their understanding and appreciation of a text by respectful, careful listening to the interpretations of others.

After their work with the exemplars, have students complete a "Reconsidering Interpretations" page, available in reproducible form in the Appendixes, to document the value of checking text and of discussing interpretations with others.

EXEMPLAR A

Reconsidering Interpretations

Title: *"Horatius at the Bridge"*

After my first reading, possibly the first part, chapter, or section, I thought that …

After reading the story I learned not to be afraid when tasks seem hard but stand up

to them like Horatius did.

_____

_____

Is my understanding as complete and accurate as possible?
As I went on reading, I came to understand …

That Horatius was also rewarded very well for his deed of saving the city.

_____

_____

_____

After carefully rereading text, especially checking sections I wondered about, I now understand that …

Horatius was a real Roman soldier in the Middle Ages and that he was the strongest

swimmer in Rome.

_____

_____

After discussing my understanding with others, I now think that …

Horatius is like Eustace in The Silver Chair *because Eustace also took on a hard task*

without complaint.

_____

_____

Reconsidering Interpretations

Title: <u>"We are Seven"</u>

After my first reading, possibly the first part, chapter, or section, I thought that …

Rebecca was a quiet girl who doesn't talk very much.

_____

_____

_____

Is my understanding as complete and accurate as possible?
As I went on reading, I came to understand …

That Rebecca was actually very talkative.

_____

_____

_____

After carefully rereading text, especially checking sections I wondered about, I now understand that …

I wondered why Rebecca was going on the train. I now understand that Rebecca was going

to go help her Aunt Miranda.

_____

_____

After discussing my understanding with others, I now think that …

People have different feelings about Rebecca. I now feel that Rebecca had a lot to say. Anne

of Green Gables is quite like Rebecca because they are both talkative. They both

were sent away from home. They both grew up to make the best of their lives, and

to be brave.

Effective Planning Strategies

Exemplars of planning strategies employed by students are useful in focusing students on discovering strategies that work best for them for different writing tasks.

Before working with the four exemplars provided, engage the class in discussion about various ways that writers plan. Some of the ways are outlined below:

- lists, which are often used in explanations, including single-paragraph ones
- webs, often used in expository writing
- story grammar (character, setting, initiating event or story problem, events or attempts at solving the problem, resolution of the problem, ending), appropriate for narrative texts
- outlines, used in expository writing (although most students prefer webs)
- flowcharts, used in expository writing that describes a sequence
- RAFTS (Role, Audience, Format, Topic, Strong verb—see pages 41–42)
- Somebody, Wanted, But, So or Somebody, Wanted, But, So, Then for narrative texts (see pages 66–67)

There are also many others, including preparing interview questions, making close observations with a notepad, and doing story maps—the list would be long.

Ask students to consider whether different writing tasks call for different strategies. Would they plan to write a business letter the same way that they would plan to write a story? The Organization section of this book recommends planning that relates specifically to RAFTS, especially format, while the B.P.D.O.G. approach, outlined in "Pre-Writing for Business Letters," works for business letters, but not for stories.

Be sure to challenge students to consider the planning strategies that work best for them. Note that Exemplar A has modified this book's suggestion of the Somebody, Wanted, But, So, Then strategy for narratives. Exemplar B presents a visual alternative for narrative planning. As a general rule, when discussing and modeling planning strategies with students, invite students to suggest practical alternatives.

The questions related to the following exemplars remind students that different writers plan differently and that it is important to discover what works best for them. However, students should also be open to learning new strategies. Research strongly argues that students who thoughtfully select strategies write better than those who don't.

Planning Strategies

The following exemplars feature the work of four students responding to this writing prompt:

> One day, while I was sitting in the front of my house, I heard a truck screech around the corner. I saw some gravel fly up as the driver stepped on the gas. Suddenly, a great big box bounced off the back of the truck and landed on the sidewalk.

Review the exemplars and respond to the questions that appear below them.

EXEMPLAR A

Somebody	Wanted	But	So
I	to take the mirror from her face	the creature wanted her to stay	I find a way to break it

EXEMPLAR B

R = Me (a nine-year-old girl)   R = Role
A = Mrs. Smith   A = Audience
F = Narrative   F = Format
T = A big box falling off a truck   T = Topic
S = Telling   S = Strong verb (purpose)

EXEMPLAR C

Title: The Country Duplicates

Setting: A country town

Characters: Me and my mom

Events: Box lands on sidewalk.
Try to open it.
Finally open it.
Duplicate inside.
Make duplicate.
It makes duplicates who try to blow up town.
Pluto blows up.

Ending: I save town from duplicates.
Send them to Pluto and pay for the damage.
The duplicates then blow up Pluto.

EXEMPLAR D

There is no address on the box.

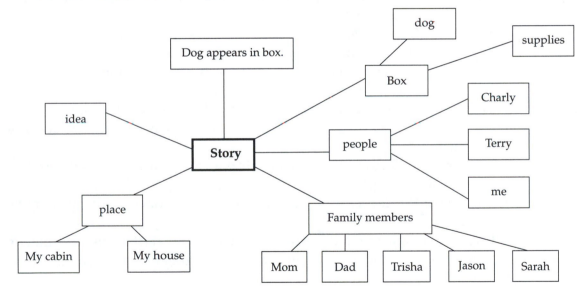

Questions:

1. a) Which of these strategies is closest to the strategy you would use to plan a story?
   b) Would you follow the strategy exactly as illustrated above or would you change it? How?
2. Specify your preferred strategy for planning to write a story.

2. Content

Effective writing includes adequate and relevant ideas appropriate for the writer's purpose and audience. The details in the composition should interest the reader and demonstrate original thinking. Exemplar-based activities in this section help students improve all of these important aspects of content:

- **Relevant and Irrelevant Detail—Informational Text** uses exemplars to emphasize that ideas in writing should clearly relate to the writer's purpose.
- **Relevant and Irrelevant Detail—Narrative Text** focuses on an identical instructional goal with narrative rather than informational text.
- **Writing Variables for Focus and Inspiration** stresses the value of thinking about role, audience, format, topic, and purpose to plan writing and to discover ideas.
- **Engaging Story Beginnings and Endings** explores specific techniques that students can use to command attention.
- **Strong Endings for Narrative Texts** challenges students to compare the endings of two stories to improve an ending in their own story.
- **Openings for Expository Texts** challenges students to compare openings of expository texts to improve their own opening lines.
- **Effective and Ineffective Topic Sentences** demonstrates how identical paragraphs in the body of a composition are richly enhanced through specific topic sentences.
- **Showing, Not Telling** teaches students the value of details that illustrate rather than just explain.
- **Titles That Work** reviews techniques used by authors to create memorable titles.
- **Playful Exemplar Activity: Off-Topic Sentence Insertions** invites students to learn the importance of relevant detail by inserting distracting detail into a text.

Relevant and Irrelevant Detail—Informational Text

By inserting a sentence that may be interesting, but still distracts from the author's focus, teachers can use exemplars to focus students on paragraph unity. Since the exemplars in this activity feature informational texts, the activity would work best for students who include irrelevant or distracting detail in their own informational texts.

To help students stay on topic in each paragraph, insert a fascinating, but distracting sentence into an exemplar. Challenge students to identify the distracting sentence.

Next, have students review a piece of their own writing to ensure a clear topical focus in each paragraph—they should cross out irrelevant or distracting details.

Exemplar A Distracting Sentence: Young people do have access to educational opportunity.

Exemplar B Distracting Sentence: While about one billion people on Earth describe themselves as non-religious, the majority of people profess a religious affiliation.

EXEMPLAR A

Age discrimination dominates as a major irritant for young people. You have to meet an age target for rights, options and privileges. Even though 16 year olds could make a rational decision about voting, only 18 year olds can vote. In addition, young people looking for a job are denied opportunities because older applicants have more extensive experience. Young people do have access to educational opportunity. Young peoples' opinions tend to be automatically dismissed even though shallow opinions can occur in all age groups. While unfair discrimination hurts innocent victims, age discrimination deserves as much attention as other forms of unfair discrimination.

EXEMPLAR B

All of us should be respectful of the sincerely held religious beliefs of others even when these beliefs are different from ours. People of different religions are often labeled as pagans, infidels, traitors, or misguided souls. Religious beliefs still get people killed in today's world. Religious fanatics believe that they are right about everything, and other religions are wrong about everything. While about one billion people on Earth describe themselves as non-religious, the majority of people profess a religious affiliation. It is helpful to be true to principles of one's faith in a way that recognizes similarities in other faiths and that explores the rich culture of other traditions. It is always lethal to condemn others just because of different beliefs.

Relevant and Irrelevant Detail—Narrative Text

Young writers often include detail that does not add to the overall effectiveness of the text. They may do this for one or more of the following reasons:
- They have been encouraged to add description which they interpret to mean description in every sentence.
- They want to fill the page.
- They elaborate a minor point and lose sight of their plan or purpose.
- They lack the skill to make logical connections.

Since the exemplar in this activity features narrative text, this activity will be most appropriate for students who include irrelevant or distracting details in their stories.

Read the exemplar on the next page with the class before asking students to cross out parts that do not add to the story. The following sentences should be crossed out:

I had black hair, golden-framed glasses and was very smart.

My eyes were dark brown.

Everybody in Calgary said that my legs were not very long.

There was a tall man with a red shirt.

His pants and shoes were completely black.

He looked so scared as a dangerous penguin was going to attack or pounce on him.

Students should then be challenged to add relevant detail.

After working with the exemplar, students should review one of their own stories to cross out detail that does not enhance their stories and to add relevant detail. Many students need to be reminded that stories require a conflict or problem that the protagonist must deal with and that the conflict must be resolved. Student writers sometimes get so carried away with irrelevant detail that they forget to resolve the story's conflict. If such is the case, have students work with the "Somebody, Wanted, But, So, Then" activity, pages 66–67.

The Undefeatable Penguin

(partial story)

One day, in Calgary, I was sitting on the gray, uncomfortable deck when suddenly I heard a truck screech that sounded like a screaming woman.

I had black hair, golden-framed glasses and was very smart. My eyes were dark brown. Everybody in Calgary said that my legs were not very long.

The truck was as huge as a one thousand-pound elephant. On the truck it said, "DANGER." It had six humungous tires.

There was a tall man with a red shirt. His pants and shoes were completely black. He looked so scared as a dangerous penguin was going to attack or pounce on him.

When the driver stepped on the gas, dark gray gravel flew up and hit my face. It hurt so much. It felt like being slapped in the face one hundred times. The pain was gone in an instant. Suddenly a giant box fell out of the big truck. It made a small crack in the cement. On the box it read, "Do Not Drop. Handle with Care."

Writing Variables for Focus and Inspiration

Exemplars effectively teach students about the importance of a writer's choices among writing variables. The word *RAFTS* represents the variables:

R   Role   From whose point of view am I writing? My own? Someone else's?

A   Audience   To whom am I writing? What is my relationship to this audience? Do I need to be formal or casual in my writing?

F   Format   What type of writing am I choosing to fulfill my purpose or has been assigned to me? In other words, am I writing a story, an expository essay, a business letter, or in some other writing format?

T   Topic   What am I writing about?

S   Strong verb   What is my purpose? What exactly am I seeking to achieve in my writing?

The following chart illustrates RAFTS.

Role	Audience	Format	Topic	Strong Verb
self	self	diary	undone homework	to justify
reporter	subscribers	article	hockey final	to inform
scientist	colleagues	report	bacteria	to warn
friend	mourners	eulogy	life of—	to honor

Have students examine Exemplar A (role of a fish) and Version B (role of an all-knowing author) to decide the advantages of each role. Students should note that the choice of a first-person role as in Exemplar A often results in a stronger voice and in richness of detail. The role selected in Exemplar A helped the student discover ideas not discovered in Exemplar B.

After work with the exemplars, challenge students to apply the RAFTS variables in their planning for a piece of writing.

Consider having the students write two versions of a narrative: one in first person and one with an omniscient role. The two exemplars for this activity provide a precedent. One student wrote both versions of the text to explore preferences and expressed preference for the first-person role.

Ol' Freddy

(written in first-person role)

How could a fish escape the constant bombardment of delectable morsels meant to rip me away from my watery world? Ah fishing, my nemesis. One memorable trip to the surface involved me with a young human named Tyler.

Tyler was a minnow human, but he had a full grown human with him. The booming voices stomping in the metal boat should have alerted me to the danger, but the wriggling worm was too much.

I resisted the first day but yesterday's large meal of stickleback provided me willpower. The second morning I was sunning in the shallows when the metal tub returned. Into the crystal waters, the bait plunged. I flicked my translucent tail and hit the hook with a mighty tug.

The minnow human pulled me to the surface and I gasped for breath. Flopping in the bottom of the metal boat I traveled to the shore. A flash of light illuminated my eyes as I gasped what I thought were my last breaths. I heard a voice say, "He's a bit small. Let's release him."

Finally the cool relief of water washed over me. I took a deep breath and reassured myself that the next time I wouldn't take the bait.

EXEMPLAR B

Ol' Freddy

Tyler and his Uncle left excitedly one Saturday for the river. Tyler's Uncle brought over the boat and they sailed out. They found a good spot that they thought Ol' Freddy would be.

They waited, and waited, and waited and waited some more. They had been waiting for up to seven hours. They got tired and went home. The next day they went to a different spot.

After two hours they were about to leave when they saw something move. Uncle Joe grabbed the rod. Ol' Freddy was fighting and wouldn't come up. Everyone grabbed the rod and pulled him up.

They went to shore and took pictures. Then they released Ol' Freddy into the lake to play another day. They had a lot of fun.

Engaging Story Beginnings and Endings

Have students examine the following openings to a story:

My cousin Lillian built a time machine. She wonders whether I'm interested in a trip.

or

I'm so excited! My cousin Lillian is taking me to the time machine that she built. She will take me anywhere that I want.

Which is the more interesting and effective opener? The second opener is superior in that it builds suspense. What is the speaker excited about? Her movement towards the time machine raises interest about what it's like.

Engage students in a discussion about techniques employed to creative effective and interesting beginnings in stories. The following chart includes effective techniques frequently employed by story writers.

Story Beginnings

- Present a brief dialogue related to the conflict.
  Example: "Dad, the water's too high!"
  My father yelled back, "Quick, paddle to shore!"

- Plunge the reader into a conflict or dramatic event.
  Example: Mr. Thorkild was the new neighbor of Sue and Tim Johnson. Late on a moonlit night, Sue and Tim noticed him burying something in his backyard. Sue inched over to her brother and asked, "I wonder what could be in the box?"

- Describe a setting to focus on movement or action related to the story's conflict.
  Example: Over 200 spectators sat in the school gym waiting for the junior boys team to appear. We hunched at the entrance doors peeking at Mr. Lumley, our coach, for a signal. Our task—to enter without tripping and to sink a basket on the way to the players' bench. I was completely petrified. As the crowd roared in response to the perky cheerleaders, I convinced myself that if I didn't fall on my face, I'd miss my shot.

- Introduce suspense or make the reader wonder about something.
  Example: It was dark already! Shelley, Cindy and I had stayed at the library too long. We decided to take the short cut home because, if we went the other way, it would be even darker before we got home. We would have to go past the house on the hill but we were not afraid. We walked quickly for about five minutes. Suddenly we heard whispering. It came from behind us.

Then have students examine the following last lines in a story about killing a deer on a hunting trip:

Alternative 1: Then I woke up! I hadn't been hunting after all.
Alternative 2: It was an exciting experience.
Alternative 3: I put away my gun and never hunted again.

Which of the three ending lines is the most effective? Remind students that "wake up" endings, illustrated by Alternative 1, are overused and should be unacceptable. Alternative 2 is a weak generalization, also overused in student story writing. Alternative 3 is much better in that it indicates how the experience of hunting has changed the character's life. It suggests that hunting was not as glamorous as the character had imagined.

Engage students in discussion about techniques employed to create interesting and effective endings to stories. The chart on page 45 includes techniques frequently used by story writers.

After the discussion, have students assess the beginnings and endings of Exemplar A and Exemplar B. Both exemplars plunge the reader into the action and both create suspense. However, Exemplar A has a superior conclusion. While both present a final reaction, Exemplar B offers an impersonal, preachy conclusion. Exemplar A is more genuine, personal, and convincing.

After working with the exemplars, students should review and revise the beginning and ending of their own stories.

Story Endings

- Tell about a final emotional response, reaction, or something learned from the experience.
  Following a series of frightening experiences on her walk home on a dark night, including being tricked into thinking that a headless creature was crushing towards her, a girl realizes how much she appreciated her brother coming to the rescue: "I'm glad my brother was worried about me and came to look for me! Now he's going to help us plan a good way to scare those boys back."

- Illustrate changes in attitudes or beliefs.
  A seven-year-old girl writes about wanting a special doll more than anything else for Christmas. Even though she knows it's expensive, she tells her parents what she wants and tells them not to worry about cost since Santa will bring it. Near Christmas, she notices a shopping bag in the storage closet. Inside the bag, she finds the doll in a box with a price tag affixed. She realizes that her parents supplied Santa's gifts at great sacrifice since the family was not well off: "The Christmas when I was eight years old was the year that I discovered the real meaning of Christmas."

- Illustrate how the events might affect the protagonist's future.
  A boy in a hospital bed overhears his doctor tell his mother that the exploding lantern that put him in the hospital has blinded him. His mother is silent and withdrawn during many visits that follow. While she tries to be reassuring, she cannot hide her tears. Finally, the boy blurts out, "I know that I'm blind." His mother sobs but tries to comfort him, "You know they have dogs for blind people."
  "Yes, I know," I reply.

- Conclude with a surprising twist.
  A boy and his father are whitewater rafting. The boy tells his father that the water is too high, but the father shrugs off the concern. In a few minutes the boy's kayak slams into a huge rock plunging him into the icy water. The boy feels himself being pulled out of the water. As his father carries the boy to their car, the boy mumbles, "I told you the water was too high."

Blizzard

Sweating, as sun beat down on my back, I was enjoying the light breeze as I soon knew winter was coming. I came home in the late evening to find my family on the porch fanning and trying to keep themselves cold. Alex stroked his short, dark hair and my little baby sister was crawling around in search of toys. Thankfully my mom emerged through the door with glasses of lemonade. I drank thirstily as it soothed my throat. Blissfully I darted into the house and looked around the quiet room and drowsily fell asleep on my warm, soft, comfortable bed.

The next morning I glanced outside, the white, pale snow was gleaming bright like a shining star. It fit perfectly with the outside scenery. I found Alex and Adrien each whipping hunks of white, icy fluff at each other. Suddenly the cold air whipped around my body and I could see nothing but blur and white. A sudden wind blew that carried the snow out into a blizzard. Rapidly, we sprinted inside.

Inside I glanced at the TV every few seconds while Adrien and Alex were cleaning up and brushing off the snow. Adrien cleaned off his hair and came to watch TV. Although the Weather Channel warned not to travel, my little sister needed to be picked up from daycare. Miserably, I put on my coat and ran outside.

The gusting wind spun all around me. Icy winds raged through the skies. Gasping, I finally stopped the car at a bridge that looked rickety, dangerous, and ancient. Small boards were smashed by rocks of ice from the blizzard. How could I get through?

Moving forward the car rocked and smashed as the front wheel burrowed into the bridge. I was sinking! I was rocketed forward and I hit my head hard. I couldn't see or move but my body told me to go to sleep.

A small bright light tickled my eyes. I thought I was dead, but I woke up as the sun rose over the dash. As I turned my side and got up I grasped the bridge's edge. Powerfully the car smashed right through the bridge deck.

Step by step I walked along the rail as I held on tight. Unfortunately it split right where I was holding it. Slipping, my death was near. I closed my eyes. As I slipped a warm sensation reached my hand and raised me up. It was Alex!

The next day as I woke the blizzard had stopped. I got up, stretched, and ran out the door all the way to the bridge. I took one last glance and thought how lucky I was to have family that cared.

The Bird and the Dog

I was taking my afternoon nap when all of a sudden I heard a loud crash! It was coming from behind the garage. I went over to see what it was and I heard a strange little voice. It was saying, "Oh, great, I can't get up, now something will eat me for sure!" What was weird was that when I saw what was making the noise it was a little blue bird. The weird part for me was that I thought birds flew over the clouds not fall into garbage cans. The most surprising things for me though, was that when I came around the corner he yelled, "Ahh, a dog. I knew my life was over!" I thought that was very odd, because dogs are friends not foe.

I replied, "I am not going to hurt you. I will help you." So I took him inside and bandaged his wing up. I kept him hidden because my owners have problems with birds. They think they're unclean.

The next day I needed to get that bird out of the house before my owners found him. So I asked him, "Would you like to go for a walk? You can ride on my back." "Sure!" he replied happily. Bad idea I figured out later. We were walking and every animal in town came racing at us. We ran home screaming our heads off. When we reached inside the house we both sighed a sigh of relief. Our troubles weren't over, because standing in front of us was Mrs. Willy my owner. "Ahhh, a bird!" she screamed. She picked up her broom and started whacking the ground like a mad woman. We escaped to my room and fell asleep. At least the bird did. I was up thinking what I should do with the bird. It finally hit me. "Smack! Ouch. I did not mean it literally." Anyway I would teach the bird how to fly.

The sun shone in my face as I thought today I will teach him how to fly. "Get up today you're going home!" I yelled. "What, I am?" he mumbled confused. I explained everything to him now we just had to do it. Together we climbed to the top of the Empire State building. We did the steps and flew. Of course he did, I did not. He flew home. And I went to the hospital. The point is, help out your friends and do not care about yourself (all the time).

Strong Endings for Narrative Texts

Student writers often struggle with effective endings for stories. The result may be the all-too-familiar "Then I woke up" ending. Discussions about techniques to conclude a narrative well are enhanced by work with exemplars.

Two versions of a story, one with an effective ending and one with an ineffective ending, help students incorporate effective endings into their own stories.

Challenge students to identify the superior ending in Exemplars A and B. Exemplar B presents an imaginative surprising twist that makes it superior to the unimaginative observation in Exemplar A. It thereby exemplifies one of the four major kinds of effective endings identified below and illustrated in the previous activity.

- Show the character's reaction to the resolution of the story's conflict.
- Include an action that shows a change of attitude or perspective.
- Present a surprising twist.
- Illustrate how the events might affect the character's future.

Review techniques frequently used by authors to create interesting endings.

Challenge students to reconsider one of their own story endings to make it more interesting and effective. One option is for students to work with a partner to consider which of the techniques for endings might work for a selected narrative; they could apply two different techniques and select the one that seems to work best.

EXEMPLAR A

Creak-Bang-Thud

I could hear owls taunting me to enter the old house. After a minute of reflection, I decided to go in.

As I opened the door, a wave of foul smelling odors reached my nose. From my pocket I produced a nose clip which I quickly put on. Horrified, I stood still because a huge crack was coming towards me. When it reached me, the ground beneath me shattered with a bang.

As I fell aimlessly, I could feel the walls closing in on me. Before I knew it, I landed on the amazingly soft floor with a thud. I groped around for my knapsack. Fear spread through my body when I realized it wasn't there. Fear changed to reality when my knapsack landed on my head. I picked it up, reached in and took out a flashlight. As I turned it on, I realized why the floor was so soft. It was pure gold dust. When I looked around I saw a treasure chest. Then I realized I had no way out, until I saw the trap door. I stuffed my pockets with gold and silver, opened the trap door and ran like crazy until I arrived home.

It was an exciting adventure.

EXEMPLAR B

Creak-Bang-Thud

I could hear owls taunting me to enter the old house. After a minute of reflection, I decided to go in.

As I opened the door, a wave of foul smelling odors reached my nose. From my pocket I produced a nose clip which I quickly put on. Horrified, I stood still because a huge crack was coming towards me. When it reached me, the ground beneath me shattered with a bang.

As I fell aimlessly, I could feel the walls closing in on me. Before I knew it, I landed on the amazingly soft floor with a thud. I groped around for my knapsack. Fear spread through my body when I realized it wasn't there. Fear changed to reality when my knapsack landed on my head. I picked it up, reached in and took out a flashlight. As I turned it on, I realized why the floor was so soft. It was pure gold dust. When I looked around I saw a treasure chest. Then I realized I had no way out, until I saw the trap door. I stuffed my pockets with gold and silver, opened the trap door and ran like crazy until I arrived home.

I will never have to ask for an allowance again!

Openings for Expository Texts

By reviewing exemplars that illustrate effective and less effective openings for expository text, students may learn to incorporate interesting openings in their own expository writing.

Ask students to review Exemplars A and B, especially the opening paragraphs, to choose the superior exemplar and to identify techniques that make it more effective. The following list itemizes techniques frequently used to create interesting introductions in expository text:

Technique	Example
A. Ask a question.	Do you feel inadequate when you speak in public?
B. State a startling fact or detail.	Few people would know how to survive if they became lost in the wilderness.
C. State a foolish or incorrect view.	Many people believe that the Internet is just for technical experts or "geeks." Nothing could be more ridiculous; everybody can benefit from using the Internet.
D. Use an effective quotation.	"We are our brother's keeper." Because human beings are at their best when they care for one another, all of us should learn first aid so that we can help in emergencies.

Exemplar A is superior in its use of a startling, attention-grabbing detail about the writer's grandfather dying of lung cancer when the writer was five years old. Exemplar B's opening statement "Children are smart too" could be stronger. Challenge students to employ one of the techniques featured in this lesson to improve the opening for Exemplar B. Then challenge students to improve the opening of one of their own expository texts.

EXEMPLAR A

When I was about five years old, my grandfather died of lung cancer. Although he had not had a cigarette in twenty years, the doctors still said that the cancer came from past smoking. Sometimes I wonder what would the world be like without cancer. What if smoking were banned? What if the discovery that cigarettes are harmful to your health had been made earlier? Would my grandfather still be alive? Maybe we would have been closer if he would have lived longer. I don't want others to be in my position or my grandfather's position. Smoking is bad for your health, and that message needs to be spread.

EXEMPLAR B

Children are smart too. We are capable of doing more than expected. Adults look down on us as if we are good for nothing sometimes, but that shouldn't be the case. Three main things that I believe that are being used wrongly on children and teens are the effects of voting, pressure and jobs. These will be explained in the following essay.

Effective and Ineffective Topic Sentences

Weak topic sentences are all too typical in expository writing. Part of the reason is that students lack experience with the form. They are more comfortable writing stories than explanations. Poor topic sentences often reflect poor planning. Use of a planning form similar to that presented on page 68 should result in more sharply focused topic sentences. In addition, many students benefit from an oral rehearsal answering this question: "What are my key points?"

Students need to learn that paragraphs focus on a single topic. While the topic sentence need not always be the first sentence, a paragraph should clearly focus on one topic, and most often a paragraph is best served by having the topic sentence first.

In the two exemplars that follow, the topic sentences are underlined. Although the topic sentences are different, the body of the paragraphs is identical—one exemplar is a degraded version of a superior student composition.

Challenge students to identify which exemplar's topic sentences offer clearer guideposts to the reader: Exemplar B is superior in its topic sentences because they clearly signal the content that follows. Students could return to Exemplar A and transform its weak topic sentences into stronger alternative sentences with beneficial results.

Exemplars A and B are also useful in reviewing effective openings for expository text. You might ask students to select the more effective introduction and to identify the technique employed. Exemplar B is superior in its startling detail: "During slavery black people were treated like animals." "This essay is about …," which is the way Exemplar A begins, is a weak opening.

After they work with the exemplars, ask students to review one of their own expository essays or paragraphs to improve the precision of the topic sentences.

EXEMPLAR A

Painful Freedoms

This is an essay about how badly black people were treated during slavery. They basically had no rights or freedoms and were considered to be property of the slave owners. Most slaves were put to work on plantations. They were ripped from their families and not given a choice. Many black slaves got whippings and were expected to obey their masters. There were many slaves that were tortured or whipped to death. Slavery should never have been part of history.

People should not be slaves. For example, in *Underground to Canada* Sims said, "Get into that wagon, girl, or I'll use my whip and teach you how to jump!" A person shouldn't be forced to do things just because of their colour. They were treated with no respect and without compassion. A slave owner didn't care if their slaves were injured or badly hurt. They were expected to labour in the fields beyond the point of exhaustion. The slaves were treated inhumanely. People should never be hurt because of another person's anger or ignorance.

There is no difference between black and white people. It is not fair that black people had to be treated and farmed like animals based on their skin colour. It was a very good thing that there were abolitionists around. It proves that there were people who didn't agree with the poor treatment of the black people. Black people are everyday people like you and me. Everyone should be able to share the same freedom.

All people were given their own free will and the slaves were forced to give theirs up and obey the slave masters. It was almost as if the white people were kings and queens and the slaves were their subjects. Life was not fair to the black slaves and knowing that slavery was wrong and the dream of freedom was what kept them going.

In conclusion, I'm sure that you would agree that slavery is a very bad thing. The way the white people treated the black people was just unacceptable. Hopefully people will learn from their mistakes and instead of focusing on our differences we should concentrate on what makes us the same. I believe that abolishing slavery was the right thing to do. After all, the black people were the ones who painfully suffered for freedom.

Painful Freedoms

During slavery, black people were treated like animals. They basically had no rights or freedoms and were considered to be property of the slave owners. Most slaves were put to work on plantations. They were ripped from their families and not given a choice. Many black slaves got whippings and were expected to obey their masters. There were many slaves that were tortured or whipped to death. Slavery should never have been part of history.

The treatment of the black slaves was inhumane and unacceptable. For example, in *Underground to Canada* Sims said, "Get into that wagon, girl, or I'll use my whip and teach you how to jump!" A person shouldn't be forced to do things just because of their color. They were treated with no respect and without compassion. A slave owner didn't care if their slaves were injured or badly hurt. They were expected to labour in the fields beyond the point of exhaustion. The slaves were treated inhumanely. People should never be hurt because of another person's anger or ignorance.

The colour of a person's skin should not colour our thoughts of them. It is not fair that black people had to be treated and farmed like animals based on their skin colour. It was a very good thing that there were abolitionists around. It proves that there were people who didn't agree with the poor treatment of the black people. Black people are everyday people like you and me. Everyone should be able to share the same freedom.

People are born with free will, and no one should take that away from them. It was almost as if the white people were kings and queens and the slaves were their subjects. Life was not fair to the black slaves and knowing that slavery was wrong and the dream of freedom was what kept them going.

Slavery was a moral evil. The way the white people treated the black people was just unacceptable. All of us should hope that people will learn from their mistakes and instead of focusing on our differences will concentrate on what makes us the same. I believe that abolishing slavery was the right thing to do. After all, the black people were the ones who painfully suffered for freedom.

Showing, Not Telling

Memorable writing shows more than it tells. Exemplars can help students learn the difference between showing and telling and the value of showing in their writing.

Challenge students to identify whether Exemplar A or B is better writing and why. Exemplar A tells about the scary first day of school and the mean teacher. Exemplar B shows scary details and the teacher's sharp opening words.

Repeat the challenge with Exemplars C and D. This time you might have students place an *S* over details that show. Since Exemplar D includes more details that show, it is superior.

Continue the activity by having students work in small groups to transform the three "telling sentences" below into showing sentences. An example is provided.
Telling: Mary was angry.
Showing: Mary stormed into the room, grabbed the telephone and slammed it into the wall.

1. The old man is very kind.
2. My friend is stingy sometimes.
3. I am sad.

Complete the exercise by having students revise a piece of their own writing to add details that show. They might mark these details with the letter *S*. Alternatively, they could work with either Exemplar B or Exemplar C to develop or complete the story with an emphasis on showing, not telling. They might mark the showing parts with the letter *S*.

Suggestion: Although this activity has focused on showing character through action, another way of showing character is through dialogue. You might want to draw students' attention to Exemplar B which shows how direct speech can reveal what characters are like. Students could review a piece of their own writing to determine whether dialogue that reveals character could be effectively added. Using sticky notes is one way for them to mark their revisions.

First Exemplar Set

EXEMPLAR A

It was my first day of school in grade six. It was quite scary going into class. Everyone I'd chatted with felt the same way. When the teacher began to speak, the entire class knew that he was mean. My friend passed me a note that exclaimed to me "Another fun year!"

EXEMPLAR B

"Get in a straight line and no talking!" As the teacher barked the orders by the school door, my classmates glanced at each other with eyes squinted and lips pressed together. When we settled into our desks, the teacher greeted us with "I mean serious business this year. There will be no nonsense." My friend passed a note that exclaimed to me "Another fun year!"

Second Exemplar Set

EXEMPLAR C

Struggling to see the road through the drifting, swirling snow, I noticed how the wind howled along the barren prairie. It was a cold February evening and I was trying to get to Juniper, a small village where my sister lived. As my mind drifted to the upcoming wedding I failed to notice the rickety bridge over the small stream. It was marked with caution signs, but the sticky snowflakes obscured my vision to a point where the signs were invisible.

EXEMPLAR D

It was a windy February evening as I was driving towards Juniper. My sister was getting married on the weekend and not even the worst weather could keep me away. The road was hard to see and I didn't see the old bridge or the caution signs at all.

Titles That Work

Focusing on titles encourages students to consider imaginative possibilities and to see the potential of titles as hooks to reader interest. Exemplars can remind students about the importance of title choice.

First, ask students to recall effective titles and discuss what makes them effective.

- It could be suspense. For example, *Who Is Frances Rain?* is the suspenseful title of a book by Margaret Buffie. It leads the reader to the story of a girl who finds a way to look into the past.
- It could be a reference to an exotic location. For example, *Galax-Arena,* the title of a book by Gillian Rubinstein, pertains to a story set in outer space on the planet Vexa.
- It could be a symbol or a metaphor, such as Virginia Ewer Wolff's title *Make Lemonade* reflects: that book concerns two young people whose courage and optimism help them overcome the adversities of ghetto life.

Have students identify strengths shared by Exemplars A and B: both create suspense and convey a character's response. Then, have them determine which is more effective. "The Mirror of Vanity" is unexpected and unfamiliar, raising questions about its meaning, while "Fluff My Cat" is a standard title.

Ask students to consider possibilities for improving on the title "Fluff My Cat." A group of students suggested the following alternatives:

- Surprise in a Box
- Cat-in-a-Box
- Curious Kitty

Of these three, "Cat-in-a-Box" may be the most effective.

Students should review titles of their own compositions to consider revisions for originality and for interest. Although students may be happy with the choices made previously, it is always worthwhile to look at writing with fresh eyes—and, of course, this choice of lesson was probably made based on seeing some weak titles.

Fluff My Cat

One glorious morning, I was playing hopscotch on the driveway when a huge ten-wheeler truck screeched around the corner. It dropped a huge box with the word "FRAGILE" posted all over it.

I slowly crept up to the box. It was much bigger than I thought.

Just then Mrs. Harper who is our neighbor stormed out of her house.

"Did you hear that?" she asked.

"Yes," I replied.

Mrs. Harper suggested we open it. Five minutes later Mrs. Harper brought a knife. We pried open the box.

The Mirror of Vanity

I looked around at my quiet street in Halifax. Maybe, there would be something interesting in the box. Maybe, there was a friend in the box. I looked around to make sure nobody was around. With not so much as a small pull I opened the box. The odor of wood filled my nose as I fanned a cloud of sawdust away. When at last I could see inside the box, a frown found its way to my lips.

Playful Exemplar Activity — Off-Topic Sentence Insertions

The occasional opportunity to make playful detrimental changes to an exemplar sometimes motivates students. The following activity challenges students to make detrimental changes to an exemplar to learn the importance of relevant content in writing. In this activity, students learn that ideas in a composition should consistently relate to the writer's purpose, or what the author is trying to achieve through the writing.

Note that the sentence in brackets, which was added to the original piece of student writing, may be interesting, but is off topic. Ask students to insert another interesting sentence that is also off topic. Have students work with partners to devise the most interesting distracting sentence.

Challenge students to identify the sentence that, if deleted, would most work against the author's purpose. Many students will see the deletion of the concluding sentence as most detrimental. The writer builds to the point about a beneficial aspect of disasters: that disasters bring people together to work towards a common goal. No other sentence in the paragraph points to the positive aspects of natural disasters.

After the activity, have students read their own compositions to revise for relevant content.

EXEMPLAR

Major natural disasters plagued the years surrounding and including the year 2005. The year preceding 2005 was a time in which many countries surrounding Sri Lanka were struck with one of the fiercest tsunamis ever recorded. Standing over eighty feet tall, a massive wall of water killed thousands of people and left years of mourning and rebuilding in its wake. (Sri Lanka is one of the Orient's prime vacation destinations.) A year later the United States of America was hit by a mighty and destructive hurricane that killed thousands of people and destroyed cities. While these disasters were catastrophic, they helped unite our world in a common goal—to help these devastated nations recover.

3. Organization

Effective writing demonstrates a clear and effective order of details with parts of the composition clearly connected. Activities in this section employ exemplars to emphasize planning as critical in achieving coherence.

- **Pre-Writing for Business Letters** promotes effective letter planning based on study of two business letter exemplars of varying strength.
- **Somebody, Wanted, But, So, Then** suggests one strong strategy that students can employ to organize the plot of a story. The *Then* element is particularly valuable in focusing attention on the theme.
- **Pre-Writing for Exposition** calls upon students to work from an exemplar to diagram the student writer's organization of an informational text.
- **Pre-Writing for Comparison and Contrast** presents two compositions by one student, one more effective than the other because the student used a Venn diagram for planning.
- **Paragraphing with Pizzazz** reminds students of the requirements as well as the flexibility involved in effective paragraphing.
- **Terrific Transition** illustrates the importance and variety of transitional devices available to the writer.
- **Text Sequencing to Learn About Transition** will especially appeal to tactile learners who can employ transitional devices to unscramble a text.
- **Playful Exemplar Activities—Paragraph Play** invites students to make harmful paragraph shifts to an exemplar to learn about the importance of organization in writing; a related activity calls for cooperative story writing, where students build a composition sentence by sentence.
- **Planning a Myth** engages students in analysis of a particular text form, that of animal myth, through study of an exemplar and in related planning to write their own animal myth.

Pre-Writing for Business Letters

In planning pieces of writing, students may find that their best friends are exemplars of the relevant types of text, or formats. By reviewing a superior and an inferior version of a type of text, such as lyric poem, story, editorial, expository essay, or business letter, students internalize features that will improve their writing.

The following pages feature two business letters completed by the same student. Challenge students to identify the superior letter and to defend their selection. Discuss effective business letter organization:

1. Introductory paragraph—clearly indicates background and purpose.
2. Middle paragraph or paragraphs—includes important details.
3. Concluding paragraph—ends with a goodwill closing.

Exemplar B follows business letter content and organization guidelines more effectively than Exemplar A. "My name is Jerry Michaels" is a weak opening. In addition, note the unconventional salutation ("Mr. Jones") in Exemplar A.

Once students have selected the preferred exemplar, have them complete a B.P.D.O.G. form for that business letter (see the reproducible page that follows). The B.P.D.O.G. strategy reminds writers to establish their purpose in the first paragraph, to include relevant details in the body of the letter, and to conclude with a goodwill closing.

Next, challenge students to revise one of their own business letters with the following criteria:

- The introductory paragraph provides background to the letter and indicates the letter's purpose.
- Middle paragraphs contain important information related to the letter's purpose.
- The letter concludes with a goodwill closing.

Students may want to employ the B.P.D.O.G. form as a pre-writing strategy for their own business letters.

B.P.D.O.G. Business Letter Planning Form

One pre-writing technique for students to learn the organization of a business letter is B.P.D.O.G.

    Paragraph One—B (background) P (purpose)

    Paragraph Two—D (details) O (operations)

    Paragraph Three—G (goodwill closing)

B

P

D

O

G

11615 – 11A Avenue
Edmonton, Alberta T2B 1K4
June 1, 2007

Mr. Jones
6700 Meadowlark Rd. NW
Edmonton, Alberta T5R 1W3

Mr. Jones:

My name is Jerry Michaels. I'm on the student council for Grant MacEwan Junior High. We are providing an assembly and lunch for the volunteers. I would really appreciate for you to come and get recognized for volunteering.

The assembly, followed by lunch, will be held on June 22, 2007. The assembly will start at 11:00 a.m. and will last about 2 hours. We would appreciate that you be at our school around 10:45 a.m. The assembly is in the gym, and the lunch is in the staff room. On the menu is turkey and fixings and for dessert strawberry shortcake. We ask that you would please reply to our main office by June 14, 2007.

I hope you will come to be recognized for volunteering for our school.

Yours truly,

Jerry Michaels

Grant MacEwan Junior High School
11615 – 11A Avenue
Edmonton, AB
T2B 1K4
January 10, 2007

Ms. L. Mulley
System Analyst
Wesjave Engineering Ltd.
#510 – 752 8 Street North
Spruce Grove, AB
T3C OR5

Dear Ms. Mulley:

It is my distinguished honour to invite you to be an honorary judge at our Science Fair. The Science Fair is being held by the student council at Grant MacEwan Junior High, and is on March 30, 2007, at 7:00 p.m.

Upon your arrival, we ask you to make your way to a gymnasium. We would greatly appreciate it if you would be at the school around 6:45 p.m.

You will be judging the top 2 projects from each homeroom for grades 7, 8, and 9. For your greatly appreciated volunteering, we will be serving refreshments after the judging is completed. We ask that you please respond to the office by March 8, 2007.

We would be greatly honoured if you will be able to judge our Science Fair.

Respectfully yours,

Jerry Michaels

Somebody, Wanted, But, So, Then

A powerful planning strategy for narratives reflects important aspects of plot: Somebody, Wanted, But, So, Then.

Somebody: central character
Wanted: character's goal
But: character's central problem or conflict
So: resolution of conflict
Then: character's reaction or realization or a surprising twist to story

Many students fail to resolve their story's conflict, which makes the *So* especially helpful. The *Then* reminds students that the ending of a story frequently points to its theme. Effective stories usually imply, but do not directly state the theme.

Have students use sticky notes to mark the *Somebody, Wanted, But, So,* and *Then* elements on their copies of the exemplar on the next page.

"The House on the Hill" illustrates successful use of the strategy:

Somebody (a young girl and her friends)
Wanted (to take a short cut home on a dark evening),
But (they encountered several frightening sights and sounds, including a headless man rushing towards them)
So (the girl's brother knocks over the headless man to reveal a boy on stilts dressed to scare the girls) and
Then (the girl realizes how much she appreciates her brother and resolves to trick those who tricked her).

Note that the *Then* points to the story's theme that we truly appreciate others when they help us in difficult situations. A reaction, a realization, or a surprising twist to conclude the story points to the theme.

Once students have worked with the exemplar, challenge them to plan a story using the Somebody, Wanted, But, So, Then strategy and then to write the story. What they may find even more useful is to revise a story already drafted, using checkmarks for the *Somebody, Wanted, But, So,* and *Then* elements. In essence, they are identifying story grammar elements, which is very useful because students often get carried away with irrelevant details and fail to resolve the conflicts their stories may have presented.

"The House on the Hill" may also be employed to consider titles, which are discussed in "Titles That Work." Can students suggest a more effective title for the story?

The House on the Hill

It was dark already! Shelley, Cindy and I had stayed at the library too long. We decided to take the short cut home because if we went the other way it would be even darker before we got home. We would have to go past the house on the hill but we were not afraid.

We walked quickly for five minutes. Suddenly, we heard whispering. It came from behind us. Turning around, we expected to see someone, but it was too dark. We hurried on, our hearts beating rapidly. As we walked along a white picket fence, an animal suddenly howled! The sound frightened us.

We could hear whispering again and another howl. I got goose bumps! It sounded too close for comfort. A door creaked in the distance and a man laughed like a hyena. This time we ran! Shelley reminded me of the house that we had passed. I really did not think it was haunted, but I thought so now!

Cindy screamed!

In the moonlight, a tall figure was coming towards us. It did not have a head! It walked kind of jerky. I could not move! All of a sudden my big brother came rushing up on his bike. He zoomed up to the headless man and knocked him down! We were surprised to see Bobby on stilts!

Out of the bushes came Tommy and Joey. They played a trick on us! I'm glad my brother was worried about me and came to look for me! Now he's going to help us plan a good way to scare those boys back!!!!

Pre-Writing for Exposition

A powerful strategy to learn about planning and organizing expository writing is to review an exemplary expository essay to focus on the structure of the essay.

The pre-writing form related to the following exemplar features a topic box in the centre, smaller boxes for subtopics, and circles for specific information related to each topic. (A reproducible version appears as an appendix.)

Have students work with the exemplar to complete the following exercise:

1. Write the essay's title in the box in the centre of the pre-writing form.
2. Identify three topics developed by the writer. Mark these subtopics in the small boxes.
3. Use the circles to indicate specific detail employed by the student writer to develop each subtopic.
4. In spaces provided at the bottom of the page, note the technique used to create interest in the introduction and conclusion.

Interesting Introductions	Interesting Conclusions
1. Ask a question or questions.	1. Answer questions posed in the introduction.
2. State startling facts.	2. Make a surprising or powerful final point.
3. State a foolish or incorrect view.	3. Warn the reader.
4. Employ an effective quotation.	4. Offer a prediction.
5. Offer a surprising twist on familiar details.	

Students may also employ the pre-writing form to plan their own expository compositions. Remind students to be flexible as they use the planning form—it is a guide only. Sometimes, as they write, students discover that they have more to say about some parts of the topic than others. The discovery may lead to further division of some of the subtopics. Obviously, all content should be consistently relevant to the central topic.

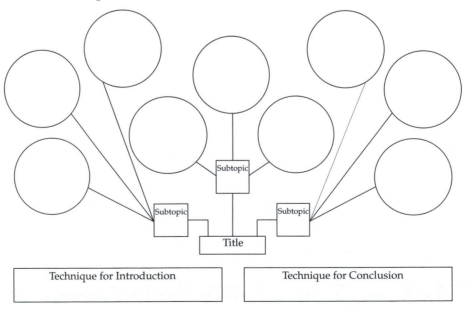

What Is Normal, Anyway?

Imagine, for a moment, that everything we take for granted today is gone. Imagine if, instead of hovercars and monobikes, people were forced to travel in slow, loud, polluting land-based vehicles capable of little more one hundred miles an hour. Imagine a life dominated by work, manual labor in positions easily filled by machines. This was the life of 2005. Put yourself in the mindset of someone living two hundred years ago as you read about how those people worked, played, and went between the two. The world of the past is waiting!

If a person went back in time to 2005, the first thing he would have to do is get somewhere. But how? He can't catch the high speed monorail, or call a hover-taxi. The most common method of transportation was a slow, land-based vehicle called an automobile, or car. These four-wheeled clunkers were driven by gasoline, a highly explosive fuel. If someone wanted to fly to his destination, a non-mach atmosphere bound "airplane" was the only option. Across the sea, large ships were the only choice, and they took days to cross. Compared to mach-speed, space capable aerojets and amphibious divers, transportation was, by today's standing, very slow. But for the citizens of 2005, it was as fast as it got.

After someone used one of these methods of transportation, where did he go? Most of the time, it was some sort of work. The manual labor which today could easily be completed by an android was done inefficiently by a person. Back then, there were actual people in stores selling their goods! While this seems a waste of a person to us today, there were no A.I. in 2005. People's lives, and lifestyles, were completely dominated by work. They made their own food—that was work—cleaned the house—also work—and drove themselves from place to place. Now, all these things are done by machines, something the workers of 2005 could only have dreamed about.

Whether working or not, most (but not all) of the people lived in cities. However, they were not like the geometric, plastic metropolis we have now. The buildings were, at most, fifty stories high, and did not extend underground for more than a few meters. The entire city was usually covered in land based roads. They were built, quite simply, for cars. In these cities, there were many places for one to buy and eat food. This food, though, was not the time released mix of vitamins and nutrients we're used to. Much of the food had little nutritional value, and barely anyone had the correct amount of nutrients each day. There were even some people who were too poor to buy food (yes, they had to buy it). Clothing was widely varied, without any resemblance to modern fashion. No-one wore a second skin in the cold, and metal on clothing was totally unheard of. While some of it looked okay, none was very successful in protecting the wearer.

Now that you've discovered what the past was like, pause to think about the present. It is different from 2005, yes, but maybe not as much as we think. After all, we were human then, too. Maybe someday, someone will look at us and say that we were underdeveloped and primitive. Maybe someday, 200 years will seem but miniscule in the great history of human civilization.

Pre-Writing for Comparison and Contrast

Exemplars can assist students to learn about effective comparison and contrast writing, one of the major text structures used in informational writing. Subjects that involve this kind of writing include social studies and science.

Use the following set of exemplars to reach two goals:

- to illustrate effective and less effective comparison and contrast writing
- to illustrate the potential of the Venn diagram as a pre-writing strategy for comparison and contrast writing

Note that the samples have been completed by the same writer, one with a Venn diagram for pre-writing, one without. The student wrote on the topic: "What would you do for a day in the summer compared to a day in the winter?"

1. Ask students to select the superior exemplar and to identify why it is superior. In choosing Exemplar B, they might note the following features:
   - Topic sentence introduces the comparison and contrast.
   - Organization makes likenesses and differences clear.
   - Transitions are clear.
   - Conclusion emphasizes key points.
2. Challenge students to use the superior exemplar to complete a Venn diagram:

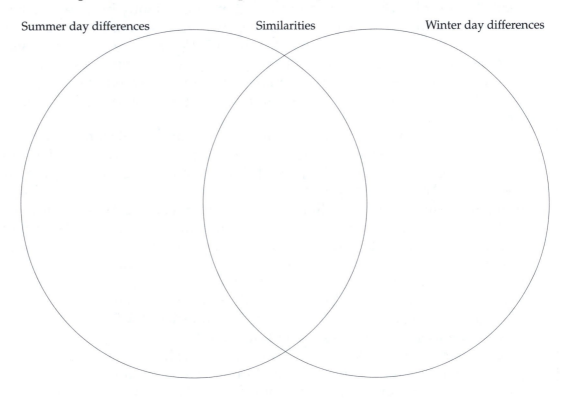

Summer day differences   Similarities   Winter day differences

3. Have students employ a Venn diagram as a pre-writing strategy for their own comparison and contrast writing.

EXEMPLAR A

A day in the summer is pretty much half over cuz I sleep till about 1–3 and then I make something for breakfast/lunch and then usually drive my dad to co-op/extra goods (I have that store) and drive home. I'll usually try and get together with friends and either go gnoming or to coffee time. (Don't ask about gnoming it's a long story) and if no ones home I'll watch tv or go on the computer till whenever I get tired and then workout for a half hour or so and then watch tv in my room until I fall asleep. In the winter it would be different because of school so I'd wake up have a shower go to school. Well, I guess I'd get dressed first. I'd come home and watch tv go on computer and do exactly the same as the summer at night. But if it was xmas holidays I'd do exactly the same as summer. How fun. He! He! He!

EXEMPLAR B

I always change what I do during the year. In the summer I'm more laid back, whereas in the winter I'm very stressed. A day in the summer and a day in the winter are very different; from when I get up, my usual activities, and when I go to sleep.

In the summer I always get up around 2 pm, so my day is half over. In the winter I always get up before 12 pm because I am in school. I am usually crankier in the winter. He! He! He!

On winter days on the weekend or during holidays I usually stay at friends' houses for the night or go walking around. Summer is quite similar to winter. I walk around and go to friends' houses. One difference in summer though is that I play soccer, which usually consumes 2–3 days a week, whereas in winter, school consumes my days.

In summer I usually fall asleep around 1 or 2 am, which results in waking up later. But in winter I have to fall asleep by 10:30 pm or else I won't wake up in the morning.

As you can see although there are some similarities, summers and winters are quite different. Summer is always great to rest and relax, but winter is great to learn and be responsible.

Paragraphing with Pizzazz

Before working with the exemplar on the next page, review paragraphing with your students.

- What is a paragraph? A paragraph is a group of sentences focused on a single topic.
- When are paragraphs effective? They are effective when information clearly focuses on the topic and develops it adequately.
- What should a writer do when the topic changes? The writer should begin a new paragraph.

The key concept of a paragraph is that it develops a separate point. Length is not the primary characteristic, as many students believe—a paragraph can be one sentence. Length is often determined by format, as in newspaper writing where the reporter's limited word count and narrow columns make short paragraphs most feasible.

With the complete class, small groups, or individuals, challenge students to show where the student writer could begin a new paragraph in the following exemplar. Strong places for new paragraphs to begin are the following:

- Sadly, this tragedy was only the first of three terrible natural disasters that attacked the civilized world that year.
- Near the end of the year in a disputed zone between the countries of Pakistan and India, a devastating earthquake occurred.

The first bulleted sentence introduces a new topic—Hurricane Katrina—so the change of topic makes the break appropriate. The second bulleted sentence introduces yet another topic—the earthquake in Pakistan and India.

These topic sentences point to a useful revision strategy. Students can check for coherence in writing by reading from topic sentence to topic sentence. Topic sentences should clearly convey essential meaning and flow from one to the other; if they do not, they should be rewritten.

After they have discussed appropriate paragraph breaks, have students revise one of their own compositions for improved paragraphing. You might have students identify and mark topic sentences and then with partners, read just the topic sentences. They could then determine how well the topic sentences lead into their paragraphs and revise accordingly.

The Year 2005

(partial selection)

Two thousand and five was a year that started with a massive tragedy—the South-Asian tsunami. The wave tore through countries such as Indonesia, Sumatra and Sri Lanka and left massive amounts of destruction in its path. Government and non-government organizations banded together and attempted to help people rebuild their shattered lives. Sadly, this tragedy was the first of three terrible natural disasters that attacked the civilized world that year. The second disaster was a hurricane. The system used to name hurricanes in 2005 was alphabetical so they named the storm "Katrina." Katrina tore through one of the most powerful countries in the world called the United States of America and destroyed much of a city named New Orleans. The government of the United States reacted slowly and many people accuse the leader of the country of only helping the rich Caucasian citizens. A popular entertainer of the day named Kanye West accused the President of "hating black people." Near the end of the year in a disputed zone between the countries of Pakistan and India, a devastating earthquake occurred. This earthquake, popularly known as Kashmir earthquakes after the name of the disputed region, garnered much response from organizations such as the Red Cross and led many people to believe that the trio of disasters signified the end of the world.

Terrific Transition

Transition is a means of connecting sentences and paragraphs to show the relationship between them. Transition helps readers stay on track. It can be achieved by referring to a previous point or employing transition expressions, such as those listed below.

Examples of Transition Expressions

Sequence: first, next, later, furthermore, last

Location: below, above, near, farther on, to the left

Similarity: likewise, similarly, again, moreover

Difference: however, in contrast, nevertheless, regardless, on the other hand

Illustration: for example, for instance, of course, to illustrate

Cause and effect: as a result, therefore, thus, consequently

In the following set, Exemplar A features clearly marked transitions. Using that exemplar, ask students to identify the value of the transitions in connecting ideas.

Then, have students identify transitions in Exemplar B, "Confidential Key."

Finally, challenge students to review one of their own compositions to identify transitions and to add appropriate ones, as needed.

EXEMPLAR A

Respect Police Officers

Reference to previous point

Reference to previous point

Transition expression

Reference to previous point

Transition expression

Transition expression

Reference to previous point

Transition expression

Police officers contribute to society in critically important ways. They do so by enforcing the law, arresting criminals, and educating citizens. Police officers make our cities safe. Without them, we would have no order and safety in our lives.

First of all, policemen and women enforce laws in a way that encourages all us to follow them. Drivers who speed, thieves who operate in quiet neighborhoods, and drug dealers who target youth are all targets of police enforcement. Without police enforcement, more people would speed, steal and deal. Our quality of life would diminish.

Moreover, we should be grateful for risks police officers take in arresting criminals. I once witnessed policemen officers breaking down a door in an apartment. In gunfire, a policeman was shot in the foot. Through the heroism of the police officers a violent thief has been removed from our midst.

Finally, police try to educate the public. Through programs such as resource officers in schools, television advertisements with safety warnings, and safety checks for car seats, police officers remind us all to make sensible choices. In challenging positive choices, police forces target young people. One city features a museum which illustrates consequences of alcohol abuse and bullying. Through the museum hundreds of young people learn about these social problems and related criminal activities.

I'm not sure I want to be a police officer. However, I respect people who are and I appreciate their work.

Confidential Key

Walking home from school, kicking a can as I did so, I hoped my life would be a little more exciting. Nothing was ever exciting. I lived in a middle-class home, with a middle-class family, with a middle-class life. As you can guess, I had a very plain name: Michael. Entirely, my name was Michael Smith. My life could be a little more exciting if I had a cool name like Spencer Sikora or something. Basically, my life was summarized in black and white, sweater-vest type commercials you see on TV. Blinded was I to the fact that in the next month my life would become much more exciting.

I tried to kick the can again but missed and fell flat on my face. As I got up, I muttered something my mother would slap me across the face for.

The can appeared to be stuck to something. Reefing on the can, I saw that the can snagged onto a jagged piece of metal. Investigating further I saw as I pulled it out that it was a very large key. No, very large won't describe it. Gargantuan or voluminous describes it better. Although it weighed what felt like 100 pounds, I dragged the key to an old man who had substantial knowledge about keys.

Finally after more than an hour of trudging, I finally reached the old man's office. I walked in with the key and as soon as he saw it, without opening my mouth, he told me to take it out back. I obeyed and when I met him out back, he went into his shed, came out with a sign, and told me that this key was the missing key that was needed to open an ancient tomb in Egypt. Many people had tried to open it before, the old man told me, but then they finally realized that a key was necessary, and I held that exact key. At first, I was skeptical, but then he pointed out some faint hieroglyphics and the irregular shape, so I began to believe it. The old man said he would talk to some historians and tell me what they thought in the morning.

Lying in bed, I reviewed my day. I had found an ancient key, possibly opening something containing gold. My name would be in newspapers, tabloids, TV! Everywhere I go the name "Michael Smith" would be staples on some sort of advertisement. Conclusively, I would get money. With all that money, I could buy anything I wanted! I could buy CD's! Sony PSPs! Nintendo DS!

Later that day, I hurried over to the old man's office. Upon thorough searching of the place, I found that he was nowhere to be found. The shed was empty, the workroom was vacant, and the office was unoccupied. I thought he must be with the historian.

My guess was wrong. He didn't come back, nor the next day. After almost a week, I still had not heard from the old man.

Unsuspectingly one dreary, Sunday afternoon, I heard a rap on my door. Eagerly I sprang up and opened it. There stood the old man. The man told me that the key was perfectly real. He required me and one family member to go with him to the tomb. My mother agreed to come with me.

On the flight there, I could scarcely believe that a week ago I was complaining of boredom. When the flight finally ended, we quickly dropped our belongings at a hotel and started driving over the cool nighttime desert.

Once we reaching the tomb, the old man hauled the key out of a sack, called me to help him lift it, and we approached the hole with the key. Then something unexpected happened; it started to get really hot. As soon as we dropped it, the key exploded like a bomb. Dumbfounded, I picked up the pieces and sighed. The key was gone forever.

On the ride home I started thinking about how boring my life was.

Text Sequencing to Learn About Transition

Text sequencing activities add the challenge of a game to students' learning about transition. The following exemplar is a newspaper article of four short paragraphs. To help students learn about transition, cut up and scramble the paragraph chunks. Students determine the logical order of the chunks. In the process, they learn that transition is key to determining the correct order.

The implicit message is that transition helps readers connect the parts of a text. Tactile learners would benefit if the chunks of text were cut up so that they could be moved around as they are placed in order. Obviously, such an approach demands more preparation time than the simple approach illustrated on the page that follows the exemplar.

The correct order of the chunks is C, B, E, A, and D.

After the text sequencing activity, have students revise one of their own compositions to improve transition. You might choose to focus on expository or informational text since that is what the exemplar is; however, since making effective transitions in narrative writing helps readers make connections, you might choose to have students improve the transitions in one of their narratives.

Teachers who have regularly employed text sequencing activities note that the approach assists students who tend to be inattentive to textual detail in their reading. Without attention to textual detail, students are unable to determine the correct sequence; therefore, text sequencing teaches a powerful reading strategy as it teaches the importance of transition.

Making a Difference

Bradford School welcomed a special guest on May 14. Ms. Madeline Scott, representing the Red Cross, spoke to an assembly of grade five and six students about tsunami relief projects in Indonesia.

Tsunami relief projects are of special interest to Bradford students because, earlier this year, grade five and six students sponsored a toy sale that raised $245 for tsunami relief .

In addition, Bradford students wrote letters to students at Inshafuddin School, a boarding school in Bana Aceh, Indonesia.

In reporting on tsunami relief efforts, Ms. Scott read the students a note from the headmaster of Inshafuddin. The headmaster thanked them for contributing to tsunami relief. The school has been supported in the purchase of textbooks and school supplies. Ms. Scott assured the classes that their caring has made a difference in the world.

Text Sequencing to Learn About Transition

In the spaces on the right, mark the correct order of the sequence of text from a newspaper article written by a student. Start with the headline as number 1.

A   In addition, Bradford students wrote letters to students at Inshafuddin School, a boarding school in Bande Aceh, Indonesia.

_____

B   Bradford school welcomed a special guest on May 14. Ms. Madeline Scott, representing the Red Cross, spoke to an assembly of grade five and six students about tsunami relief projects in Indonesia.

_____

C   Making a Difference

_____

D   In reporting on tsunami relief efforts, Ms. Scott read the students a note from the headmaster of Inshafuddin School. The headmaster thanked them for contributing to tsunami relief. The school has been supported in the purchase of textbooks and school supplies. Ms. Scott assured the classes that their caring has made a difference in the world.

_____

E   Tsunami relief projects are of special interest to Bradford students because, earlier this year, grade five and six students sponsored a toy sale that raised $245 for tsunami relief.

_____

Playful Exemplar Activities — Paragraph Play

The activity involving the exemplar "A Profession Without Equal" challenges students to move one paragraph to harm the flow of the composition. The exercise underlines the importance of transition in linking content in a composition.

Which paragraph movement would do the most damage? Movement of the fourth paragraph in the exemplar would do the most damage because the content links directly to the content in the third paragraph. The writer suggests that education is important for making a living, but is even more important for learning to live a good life. This critical point loses impact if the fourth paragraph is moved.

Another playful activity to emphasize the importance of organization is cooperative story writing.

Begin by giving a small group or partners a story opener, such as one of these:

- One fine day at the end of September when we were harvesting pumpkins on the back 10 acres of my grandfather's farm . . .
- Part of growing up is learning not to let others take advantage of you. For example, . . .
- It was the most frightening night of my life. I was walking home alone from the library when suddenly . . .

Have students pass the pencil, with each adding a relevant sentence until the story is completed. Each student's contribution must build on the previous student's ideas to create an organized whole.

Once the stories are finished, invite a member of each group to read the group's story to the class. Have class members assess whether the story stays focused, and if it does not, determine where it loses focus.

A Profession Without Equal

Teaching is without doubt a profession without equal. Teachers have a specific role in helping and encouraging students to learn effectively. While teaching empowers students to earn a good living, more importantly it helps students learn how to live well.

Not everyone can be a teacher. The great teachers know exactly how to explain concepts to reach different skills levels. Teachers have a knack of knowing how to interest different students so that learning is tangible for all. Teachers notice when someone is not learning. They are there to offer a nudge and an encouraging word. Unless you are flexible and sensitive you should not be a teacher.

In a competitive world education opens opportunity for those who learn. Teachers help students connect their learning to future employment realities. For example, computer skills may well lead students to challenging video programming employment and even movie making. Teachers help students figure out their talents so students can take courses related to employment goals and interests.

More importantly, teachers help students learn the values and attitudes of good citizenship. Teachers demonstrate that hard work, compassion and team work are more important than amassing a fortune. When teachers challenge students to do their best, and to think of the needs of others they are helping students develop attitudes that bring true satisfaction in life.

Teachers do not equal other professions in income. However, teachers are unequalled in influence.

Planning a Myth

Exemplars can be used to explore forms of writing. In this activity, students gain a better understanding of myths by deconstructing one written by a student and then creating their own.

Myths are tales that explain natural occurrences in the world, such as the idea in Greek mythology that thunder and lightning result from the anger of Zeus. Myths that explain natural events are common to many cultures. Often, these myths explain how animals possess certain characteristics or why they behave as they do. For example, the Australian Aboriginal myth about how the kangaroo got its tail explains an important characteristic of a familiar creature; the North American Native myth "Rabbit the Hunter" explains why many rabbits turn brown in the summer.

Animal myths personify animals. They usually end with direct statements about why the animal looks and behaves as it does.

As part of the study of myths, teachers frequently assign students the task of writing a myth to explain a natural event or an animal's characteristic. In planning an animal myth, students typically work backwards from the feature of the animal that they wish to highlight. They then create a tale to explain how the feature came to be.

Have students read the exemplar "How the Raccoon Got Its Mask." Ask students to employ these headings to note the organization of the animal myth:

Animal _____

Characteristics of the Animal to Be Illustrated _____

Related Plot:

Brief Background Information _____

Event Related to a Challenge, Conflict, or Problem _____

_____

Important Events in Story _____

_____

Climax or Most Important Event Pointing to the Explanation About Why the Animal Has the Important Characteristic _____

_____

After work with "How the Raccoon Got Its Mask," students may use the headings to plan their own animal myths.

How the Raccoon Got Its Mask

There once lived a raccoon who was brown and black and had a striped tail. This wasn't any normal raccoon. This raccoon could talk and run on its hind legs. But the activity that he did best was stealing.

One night while he was out prowling he made up a plan to steal the forest bank's gold. Somehow the police found out about his plan and arrested him. He said in his mind, "This is the last straw."

When he finished serving his time, he vowed never to sleep again until he had stolen every penny from the bank where he had been caught! After a month and a half of no sleep he finally stole every penny from the bank as he had promised. As he walked into his home with the bank's gold in a sack, he looked into the round hall mirror on the wall. Around his eyes his fur was so dark from lack of sleep, it looked like a mask.

He got so excited. "Now none of the forest police will ever see my shiny eyes and never catch me again!" boasted the raccoon to himself. So that is how the raccoon got its mask and why every raccoon in the world prowls at night.

4. Sentence Variety

Writers achieve effective sentence variety by varying the beginnings of sentences and the type and length of sentences. Activities in this section illustrate how exemplars teach that varied sentence patterns add interest to a text as they show the relationships between ideas in the sentences.

- **Complex Sentences** focuses on the various ways writers can begin sentences without resorting to a basic subject-verb structure.
- **Sentence Combining for Interest and Clarity** requires students to determine sentences that can effectively be combined in an exemplar.
- **Sentence Combining to Show Relationships** invites students to consider options for adding complexity to sets of simple sentences—and more clearly showing relationships between ideas.
- **Varied Sentence Beginnings** reinforces learning about options to begin sentences effectively.
- **Varied Sentence Types** reviews declarative, interrogative, imperative, and exclamatory sentences. Students consider how use of these sentence types can add variety to a text.
- **The Power of Short Sentences** highlights to students the speed and action implied by related, short sentences.
- **Playful Exemplar Activity — Simplifying the Complex** underlines the often detrimental effect of employing simple sentences to the exclusion of complex sentences.
- **Sentence Structure and Word Choice** extends students' thinking about sentence options to word choice, a topic that will be developed in the next section.

Complex Sentences

Sentences typically begin with the subject. For example: The thief crept into the room. He stole the television.

Sentence variety is desirable, however. Sentence variety ensures that the writer's sentences are not tiresomely alike. It can also add life and interest to writing. One way to achieve sentence variety is to include complex sentences that begin with something other than the subject.

Creating Complex Sentences

The correct use of subordinate clauses, participles or participial phrases, and prepositional phrases creates complex sentences. A subordinate clause contains a subject and a predicate, but does not express a complete thought on its own; therefore, it needs to be attached to a principal clause in a sentence. Here is an example, with the subordinate clause at the beginning and principal clause after the comma: "Although it is raining today, I still intend to golf." A participle is a verb form that can work as an adjective, such as *rising* in *rising expectations;* it can also be expressed as a phrase, as in *creeping into the room.* A prepositional phrase is a group of words that work as a unit, but do not contain a subject or predicate: an example is *in the garden.* A prepositional phrase can function as an adjective or as an adverb, as the third example below shows.

Note that each of the following sentences is complex because of the effective use of a subordinate clause, a participial phrase, or a prepositional phrase—two short sentences have been combined without using *and, but,* or *so* to add interest.

- After the thief crept into the room, he stole the television.
- Creeping into the room, the thief stole the television.
- Into the room the thief crept before he stole the television.

Model the creation of complex sentences for the class.

Students can learn these patterns even if they do not understand the grammatical terminology. Ask the students to choose the exemplar from the following set that best illustrates complex sentences. Then, have students identify benefits of complex sentences:

- They demonstrate the relationship between ideas.
- They add variety and interest.

Note, though, that too many complex sentences will not yield sentence variety. Sentence variety depends on including complex sentences with simple sentences and compound sentences—that is, two complete main ideas usually joined by *and, but,* or a semi-colon. (An example of a compound sentence is as follows: "The day was sunny and the children were excited about the wiener roast.")

Have students contrast Exemplars A and B to determine which employs complex sentences more effectively. Then, prompt them to study Exemplar B, which has the best examples of complex sentences. Challenge students to improve it by varying the complex sentences. Possible changes include these:

- "It was the night before Halloween. As I walked down the alley toward my home, a strange thing happened."
- "Right in front of me, standing on its hind legs, stood a grizzly bear."

The sentence above is called a periodic sentence. Note that it commands attention and builds suspense by saving the critical point for the end of the sentence—typically, sentences begin with the key point.

Finally, ask students to review one of their own compositions to identify complex sentences and to add appropriate complex sentences. You might also have them identify any periodic sentences and to create at least one such sentence. As with all sentence patterns, though, periodic sentences will lose their impact, if overused.

EXEMPLAR A

One night I was walking down the alley to my home. A strange thing happened. It was the night before Halloween and a cold breeze was in the air. I just came back from a friend's house and it was nine o'clock p.m. I was half way to my house when I heard a rustling in the bushes. I had some time left so I decided to investigate. I walked through the bushes, and through some trees. I saw a small chipmunk in front of me. I looked at it sweetly and turned around. I saw a giant grizzly bear stand on its hind legs.

EXEMPLAR B

One night as I walked down the alley toward my home, a strange thing happened. A cold breeze chilled the air on this night before Halloween. Returning from a friend's house, I noticed that it was nine o'clock. I was half way to my house when I heard a rustling in the bushes. Since I had time left, I decided to investigate. Through the bushes I walked. Before me chattered a small chipmunk. I looked at it sweetly and turned around. Right in front of me a grizzly bear stood upright on its hind legs.

Extension:

Once you identify the exemplar with the best examples of complex sentences and see how complex sentences can contribute to sentence variety, look at that exemplar again. Consider whether reordering any of the complex sentences or changing them to simpler sentences would make the piece of writing more effective. What might you do?

_____

_____

_____

_____

_____

_____

_____

_____

_____

_____

Sentence Combining for Interest and Clarity

Before beginning sentence combining work with the next exemplar, engage students with these examples:

1. The class was late for the assembly. The assembly had not started.
2. Once there was a tiny village in Mexico. Very few people lived there.
3. A little seashell lived by the sea. His name was Herman. He was a very happy seashell.
4. I'm very serious about solving crimes. Don't mess with my equipment.
5. Halfway through French class there was an interruption. The fire alarm sounded.

Review options for complex sentence structure, introduced in the previous exercise.

- You can begin with a subordinate clause, possibly marking a longer one with a comma. Example: "Since no one showed up for the meeting, I made the decision on my own."
- You can begin with a participial phrase which may be followed by a comma. Example: "Gasping for breath, he stopped."
- You can begin with a prepositional phrase, possibly marking it by a comma. Examples: "To make progress, one must work hard." "In the morning we will begin our work."

Ask students to create as many feasible sentence combinations as possible for each of the five numbered sentence groups. As you challenge students to develop combinations for each, you can turn the exercise into a game by setting a timer for about two minutes per number.

After the exercise, have students rewrite the exemplar that follows by combining at least four sentences; then, have them review one of their own compositions to identify sentences that could be beneficially combined and to do so. Keep an eye out for students inserting a period after a subordinate clause, for example: "Since the guest of honor is here. The party can begin." If you find any students creating such sentence fragments, it may be beneficial to have a mini-lesson to remind them that a comma would be more appropriate after a subordinate clause or phrase at the beginning of a complex sentence.

Mysterious Box

I walked over to the big box. I was very curious about what was inside.

There was a little hole in the box, and I decided to take a peek. Unfortunately, it was too dark to take a look. The box was very, very big.

I ran to my mom and asked if I could open the box. My mom said maybe after lunch. It was lunchtime so I ate two hotdogs. After, I pulled the enormous, heavy box into my yard. My mom said I was strong. My mom got a screwdriver and we unscrewed all the bolts. I was excited to see what was inside with my mom. It was a box full of stacked one-hundred dollar bills. When my mom saw the cash she almost fainted. I helped her back to her feet. My mom and I were millionaires. My mom and I were very excited and happy.

The next day my Mom and I loaded all the money in the truck. My mom and I drove to the bank and put our money in our savings account. My mom and I drove back to our house. My mom and I celebrated by watching a movie. We had lots of pop, popcorn and candy. My mom and I were very happy and never went bankrupt.

Sentence Combining to Show Relationships

Young writers often write a succession of simple sentences, many of which begin with such words as *I, he, they, the,* and *she.* These students benefit from the modelling of sentence combining, work with exemplars, and revision of their own writing.

In the following exemplars, numbered sentences are simple sentences. Challenge students to effectively combine pairs of simple sentences to create complex sentences. For instance, since three simple sentences in Exemplar A are marked *1,* students should correctly combine these three marked sentences in a single sentence. Remember that sentence combinations that use *and, but,* and *so* are not allowed—these words create compound sentences rather than the targeted complex sentences.

Below are the student writer's original complex sentences. While these are feasible, many other possibilities are, as well.

Exemplar A

1 Once the robot noticed me rush into the forest, he chased me, scaring the life out of me. *2* Living there for three days, I was sure the robot had abandoned the forest. *3* As I emerged from the forest, I noticed my half-obliterated house.

Exemplar B

1 Internet access that is faster today than it was when it was first invented has been enhanced by video cameras. *2* While vehicles have luxury item such as CD players, they did not have these items several years ago. *3* While telephones were once attached to walls, modern telephones are portable with video features.

After the exercise, challenge students to review one of their own compositions to identify complex sentences and to add appropriate complex sentences.

EXEMPLAR A

1 The robot noticed me rush into the forest. *1* The robot chased me. *1* He scared the life out of me. I hid in a cave. He never found me.
2 I lived there for three days. *2* I was sure the robot had abandoned the forest.
3 I emerged from the forest. *3* I noticed my half-obliterated house. No house in town was unscathed.

1. _____

_____

2. _____

_____

3. _____

_____

EXEMPLAR B

Technology has improved our lives. *1* Internet access is faster today than when it was first invented. *1* Internet has been enhanced with video cameras. Automobiles have also changed. *2* Vehicles have luxury items such as CD players. *2* Vehicles did not have these items several years ago. In addition, telephones are definitely different than they were in earlier times. *3* Telephones were once attached to walls. *3* Modern telephones are portable and have video features. Previous generations would be in awe of what we take for granted.

1. _____

_____

2. _____

_____

3. _____

_____

Varied Sentence Beginnings

The exemplar "Life on Earth in 2005" demonstrates sentences that usually begin with a subject. The writing will be more interesting and the content more clearly connected by varying the sentence beginnings. As a whole-class, small-group, or individual student exercise, have students underline the sentence beginnings; then, have students change at least five of them to add variety and interest. Students may add a few words to improve the variety and clarity of the sentences or may change the order of the sentences. Of the following sentences, the first and third include a few added words; the second has changed word order, which is another possibility:

1. Although silly people back then thought that they had to build colossal mansions, we use housing space much more efficiently. (paragraph 4)
2. Since they did not have auto-cookers as we do, in 2005, simple earthlings used freeze dried food. (paragraph 3)
3. In 2005, people used rocket ships only for research trips to the moon. (paragraph 2)

After the exercise, challenge students to review one of their own compositions to underline sentence beginnings, and if most sentences begin with the subject, to add variety to sentence openers.

"Life on Earth in 2005" also serves to review transition, discussed in "Terrific Transition." Have students identify transition devices and suggest other possibilities for transition.

Life on Earth in 2005

Life 200 years ago was very different than today. Many inventions that help us today did not exist back then.

For one example, earlier transportation methods were very primitive. They only used rocket ships for research trips to the moon. They wouldn't understand the concept of a body beamer. People walked on the ground of Earth; they did not go through chutes in the air.

The making of food back then was also different. In 2005, simple earthlings seldom used freeze-dried food. They did not have auto-cookers as we do. They had to go to the supermarket to buy food. We select from computer lists for instant delivery.

The 2005 houses and buildings were all on the ground. They did not have floating buildings. Some houses were made with wood. Silly people thought they had to build colossal mansions. We use housing space much more efficiently.

In addition, their lifestyle was extremely different than ours. Most of the time, people were in a hurry. The adults had to go to a building to work. The kids had to leave home to go to school. They did not have many online schools and online offices. How backward! They would have to make a lunch. They would eat lunch at work or school. Their pastimes included books. We read online texts.

They also used metal circles for currency. They also used pieces of paper. We simply use virtual credit for all the amazing products and services available to us.

In 2005, if anyone committed a crime, they would be hunted down by the police in person. They did not have embedded computer chips that monitor us when we do wrong. The people that committed the crimes were then taken to court where judges would determine if the suspect was guilty or innocent. Our computer monitoring provides instant judgment and sentencing.

We should be very pleased with the progress we have made in 200 years!

Varied Sentence Types

Exemplars of student writing can help students learn that varying sentences types represents another way to add interest to writing. Review the variety of sentence types with students:

- declarative (making a statement)
- interrogative (asking a question)
- imperative (stating a command)
- exclamatory (expressing strong emotion)

Most sentences are declarative.

Challenge students to identify interrogative, imperative, and exclamatory sentences in Exemplars A and B and to insert appropriate punctuation. Students should make the following changes and classifications.

Exemplar A

1. "But, Mom! This is supposed to be a vacation," Dylan angrily complained. (exclamatory)
2. It wasn't fair! (exclamatory)
3. Didn't anyone care about him? (interrogative)

Exemplar B

1. "Wow! An academy award!" he exclaimed running his finger over the long sculpture. (exclamatory)
2. "Have you found my Oscar?" Grandma chuckled as she stepped through the trap door. (interrogative)
3. "Bring it to me," she said. (imperative)

Have students review one of their own compositions with large sticky notes to mark places where a sentence type might be changed. Their revisions might be marked on the sticky notes. If their samples illustrate varied sentence types, they could use the sticky notes to label the sentence types.

EXEMPLAR A

But Mom This is supposed to be a vacation Dylan Andrews loudly complained into the huge hunk of metal that his grandma called a phone He swiftly hung up and angrily slumped down into a rickety rocking chair and let out loud, exasperated groans It wasn't fair Didn't any one care about him This was his last day off during Easter vacation and his parents made him spend it at his grandma's house while they met with their lawyer about getting a divorce.

EXEMPLAR B

The attic smelt of old clothes and dusty pieces of furniture Dylan coughed loudly as he found it hard to breathe in such an atmosphere He started cleaning by the window Dylan opened a huge box and gasped at what he saw Wow An Academy Award he exclaimed running his finger over the long sculpture

Have you found my Oscar Grandma chuckled as she stepped through the trap door. Bring it to me she said.

The Power of Short Sentences

While students should learn the value of complex sentences, including sentences that do not always begin with the subject, they should also learn that a series of short sentences sometimes suits the author's purpose. When authors wish to suggest quick action, often in description, a series of short sentences conveys speed. Sports stories or articles and action or adventure stories often use the technique. *Crossing the Line* by A. D. Fast is an example of a novel that employs short sentences to suggest quick action.

Exemplars A and B are two versions of a student's description of a volleyball game. The first six sentences are identical in these exemplars. However, starting with the seventh sentence (marked with three stars ***), Exemplar A, which was created to contrast with Exemplar B, emphasizes complex sentences. The student writer's original text, Exemplar B, emphasizes a series of short sentences.

Ask students to compare the endings of the two versions to determine why Exemplar B is more effective in meeting the author's purpose.

After the activity, have students complete a description to suggest speedy movement or to locate a writing sample that would benefit from a series of short sentences and to implement the short sentences.

EXEMPLAR A

Volley

The loud, enthusiastic crowd bursts into an uproar, filling the stale smelling gym with noise. People on the sidelines bob up and down, up and down cheering on the players. The home team drills the ball over the net, driving the herd of fans into utter mayhem. Beads of sweat dripped down the players' faces. Six hot, perspiring bodies scatter throughout the court, ready for anything that is sent their way. They slide to the right and then to the left, quick and swift like a random lightning bolt. The players' look is one of pure concentration and determination like that of a puma ready to pounce. *** As goose bumps sprout on the spectators' arms, the crowd shuffles. They know that the next point wins. When the server strikes the ball over the net, a hush falls over the crowd. Bump, set, spike, the ball is forced downwards, moving at missile speed towards the gym floor. THUD! As soon as the ball strikes solid ground, the gym erupts and cheering fans and team members dance, hug and shout. Ahhh, the sweet taste of victory!

EXEMPLAR B

Volley

The loud, enthusiastic crowd bursts into an uproar, filling the stale smelling gym with noise. People on the sidelines bob up and down, up and down cheering on the players. The home team drills the ball over the net, driving the herd of fans into utter mayhem. Beads of sweat drop down the players' faces. Six hot, perspiring bodies scatter throughout the court, ready for anything that is sent their way. They slide to the right and then to the left, quick and swift like a random lightening bolt. The players' look is one of pure concentration and determination like that of a puma ready to pounce. *** Goose bumps sprout on spectators' arms … Next point wins. The server strikes the ball over the net. A hush falls over the crowd. Bump, set, spike, the ball is forced downwards, moving at missile speed toward the gym floor. THUD! The ball strikes solid ground. The gym erupts! Cheering fans and team members dance, hug and shout. Ahhh, the sweet taste of victory!

Playful Exemplar Activity — Simplifying the Complex

The following activity underlines the importance of sentence variety in compositions by having students note the frequently detrimental effect of including too many simple sentences to the exclusion of complex sentences.

Instruct students to rewrite every sentence in the exemplar as a simple sentence. Then ask students to comment on the effects—loss of interest and lack of connection between ideas. The simplifying exercise should illustrate that the relationship between parts is not as clear in the simple sentences as it is in the complex sentences.

You may extend the activity by having students rewrite one of their own paragraphs to change complex sentences into simple sentences and, once again, to note the effect.

Your work with students might focus on the value of complex sentences. Suggest that students look up the word "complexity" in their dictionaries. Dictionary entries will indicate that complexity has to do with something of connected or interwoven parts. *Complex sentences* is not just a dreary label used by teachers and grammarians. Effective complex sentences show how ideas and parts are connected.

Finally, ask students to revise one of their own compositions to ensure sentence variety.

EXEMPLAR

The people of the twentieth century were not always peaceful. To dominate others, they used small metal objects called bullets in shooting machines called pistols and rifles. Primitive by our standards, the tank was one of their greatest war machines. With huge cannons, tanks could blast through almost any defence. When tanks appeared, defenders dispatched flying machines called helicopters. Fast and very maneuverable, the helicopter was armed with missiles and barbaric machine guns. Typically, armed helicopters dominated battles with tanks.

Text in simple sentence form:

_____

_____

_____

_____

_____

_____

_____

_____

_____

_____

_____

_____

_____

_____

_____

_____

_____

_____

This exemplar shows how teachers can focus on two or more aspects of writing. Many teachers have discovered that multi-faceted revision activities with exemplars work most effectively when students have already worked with exemplars with a single outcome focus, such as content or voice. If students are unfamiliar with language that describes effective writing, it is probably best to do single-focus exemplar work first. Previous activities in this book each focus on one main aspect of effective writing. When it is decided to address a combination of traits, the choice of traits should be determined by looking at the needs reflected in students' writing or their goals for improvement.

Exemplar A challenges students to consider vocabulary choices in items marked *1* and to consider options for combining the sentences marked *2*.

After work with the exemplar, ask students to compare their choices with those made by the author of the original text, which appears as Exemplar B.

Students can then revise a piece of their own writing to improve specific word choices and to ensure that sentences are varied.

Keeping Out the Mongols

The Great Wall of China, built along the northern border of China to defend against Mongol *1a* _____ from the north, was finally completed three days ago under the command of Emperor Qin Shi Huangdi. Extremely *1b* _____, millions of slaves were forced to build a 4,000 mile-long wall. The Emperor linked old walls, some as old as 400 BC, with the new and unified Great Wall of China. Also known as the Wall of Ten Thousand Li, the wall stretching across the country from Mount Jethi to Lin Tao. Qin Shi Huangdi has made an amazing accomplishment by building one enormous wall to defend the Chinese people.

2a The wall was constructed by overworked and abused slaves. *2b* It was mostly build out of rammed earth and beaten clay. Casualties number about 1,000,000 slaves whose deaths resulted from beatings and endless labor. The 4,000 mile-long wall is wide enough on top for ten men or six horses to march side by side. In order to surely keep enemies away, the wall was made 25 feet high. China's Emperor succeeded in creating an amazing wall but cruelly forced innocent people into severe slavery, even death.

The efficiency of the wall is undoubtedly extremely helpful to China's military defense. Almost impossible to scale, the wall effectively defended against enemies. Adding to the strength of the military and the wall is a perfect communication system to warn military squadrons of attacks. When a soldier spots enemies, he immediately activates the smoke and fire signal to alert fellow soldiers along the wall and the invaders are stopped. Emperor Qin Shi Huangdi quoted, "Perseverance is the key to doing great deeds like this for our country."

Keeping Out the Mongols

The Great Wall of China, built along the northern border of China to defend against Mongol marauders from the north, was finally completed three days ago under the command of Emperor Qin Shi Huangdi. Extremely overburdened, millions of slaves were forced to build a 4,000 mile-long wall. The Emperor linked old walls, some as old as 400 BC, with the new and unified Great Wall of China. Also known as the Wall of Ten Thousand Li, the wall stretching across the country from Mount Jethi to Lin Tao. Qin Shi Huangdi has made an amazing accomplishment by building one enormous wall to defend the Chinese people.

Constructed by abused and overworked slaves, the Great Wall was mostly built by rammed earth and beaten clay. Casualties number about 1,000,000 slaves whose deaths resulted from beatings and endless labor. The 4,000 mile-long wall is wide enough on top for ten men or six horses to march side by side. In order to surely keep enemies away, the wall was made 25 feet high. China's Emperor succeeded in creating an amazing wall but cruelly forced innocent people into severe slavery, even death.

The efficiency of the wall is undoubtedly extremely helpful to China's military defense. Almost impossible to scale, the wall effectively defended against enemies. Adding to the strength of the military and the wall is a perfect communication system to warn military squadrons of attacks. When a soldier spots enemies, he immediately activates the smoke and fire signal to alert fellow soldiers along the wall and the invaders are stopped. Emperor Qin Shi Huangdi quoted, "Perseverance is the key to doing great deeds like this for our country."

5. Word Choice

Words should be precise and accurately used in a composition. In stories, poems, and descriptions, words should also be colorful and evocative. This section employs exemplars to nudge student thinking about appropriate and effective word choice.

- **Cloze for Colorful Vocabulary** invites students to insert appropriate colorful verbs into texts.
- **Precise and Imprecise Word Choice** employs two versions of a text for students to assess the precision of word choice.
- **The Vocabulary Thing** challenges students to add color to their writing by seeking replacements to the word *thing*.
- **Colorful Choices** requires students to choose a more colorful option from word pairs and to insert other effective word choices into a text.
- **Verb Challenge** reinforces learning about effective verb choice in context.
- **Assessing Word Choice** employs a rubric for students to rate word choices in an exemplar and in one of their own compositions.
- **To Be or Not to Be** focuses students on colorful alternatives to the verb *to be* and in the effectiveness of active rather than passive voice.
- **Adding Rich Details** emphasizes how vocabulary choices can create colorful detail in stories.
- **Choices in Context** reminds students that straightforward word choices are sometimes most appropriate as students consider effective word choices in the context of an exemplar.
- **Playful Exemplars Activity — From Descriptive to Dull** engages students in noting detrimental effects of transforming five descriptive words to dull, ordinary words.

Cloze for Colorful Vocabulary

One of the most effective methods to help students think about vocabulary choices is to create cloze exercises—passages with selected words omitted. As they consider words that would fit, students learn about the importance of precise, connotative vocabulary.

Exemplar A is a paragraph with four key verbs omitted. In sharing the student writer's words, emphasize that other colorful choices will work as well:

1. gazed
2. responded
3. dropped
4. drifted

Exemplar B is a paragraph with six verbs omitted. Challenge students to suggest three replacements for each missing word. Have them trade with a partner and rewrite the piece using the best words.

The author's rather weak original choices are as follows:

1. left
2. saw
3. found
4. moved
5. opened
6. changed

After the exercise, challenge students to reread one of their own compositions to circle tired words and insert more descriptive alternatives.

Teachers have noted that the creation of cloze exercises focused on vocabulary choices is quick and effective. In work with colleagues, you may discover that your creation of learning resources with exemplars gets a boost when you begin with vocabulary cloze exercises.

EXEMPLAR A

Zoe 1._____ into Lightning's chestnut colored eyes. She

whispered "Good-night" to her buckskin horse. Lightning 2._____

with a soft nicker. With a slight smile, Zoe exited the paddock and entered her

house. She 3._____ on to her bed with a small thump and

4._____ into sleep.

EXEMPLAR B

One day little Lisa 1._____ the house to play when she

2._____ a crystal and a book. She had no idea that she had

3._____ a magic crystal. She opened the book and said, "Hocus

pokus." Suddenly the ground 4._____ and there was a blinding

light. When Lisa 5._____ her eyes she wasn't Lisa anymore. She

was 6._____ to a unicorn.

Precise and Imprecise Word Choice

By rewriting a text characterized by precise and colorful word choices to substitute imprecise, vapid vocabulary, teachers create a powerful resource to instruct students about vocabulary.

In the following set of exemplars, Exemplar A features harmful vocabulary substitutions. Engage students in line-by-line comparative reading of Exemplar A and Exemplar B, that is, read line 1 in Exemplar A followed by line 1 in Exemplar B. Have students chart different vocabulary choices as they read. Line 1 has been completed below:

	Vocabulary Choices	
Line	Exemplar A	Exemplar B
1	ancient artifacts	stuff
2		
3		
4		
5		
6		
7		
8		
9		
10		
11		
12		
13		

Engage students in comparing the lists in order to stress the importance of precise, colorful vocabulary.

After the work with exemplars, prompt students to review one of their own compositions to improve word choices.

EXEMPLAR A

The Sandpit Setback

1 Ever thought about digging up ancient artifacts in your sandbox? *2* Well, I doubt when this local landowner let her children play in a nearby sandpit, she wasn't expecting them to dig up ancient history! *3* The children uncovered what seemed to be a set of stone tools and other artifacts near a local sandpit just outside a small community in Alberta. *4* Soon afterwards, the nearby Museum was contacted and experienced archeologists investigated and excavated the site. *5* The artifacts were removed from the pit and moved to the Museum for closer examinations. *6* It has been decided that the artifacts will soon be on display to the public after the study so that people can enjoy the history of their great land.

7 After long, continuous examinations, archeologists determined the artifacts were a variety of stone tools for cutting and scraping. *8* In addition, they found the remains of a shelter and evidence of a fire pit. *9* However, the stone used for the tools were not common to the area and it is estimated that the artifacts found were from travelers long ago for it appears that the site had been used many times before its destruction. *10* It could also be an area for recreation, parties and even overnight camp outs and the archeologists believe that the destruction of the area was caused by mud during a large flood.

11 The sandpit is still closed to the general public for the archeologists continue to excavate the site in hopes of finding more evidence of human activity. *12* "For right now, the basic discoveries have been made and archeologists will not lose sleep on this matter!" reported an archeologist who works for the Museum. *13* For more information on recent artifact discoveries, check out the Museum's Website at http://www.museum/artifacts.com/.

The Sandpit Setback

1 Ever thought about digging up stuff in your sandbox? *2* Well, when this landowner let her children play in a nearby sandpit, she did not expect them to find something! *3* The children found what seemed to be a set of tools and other things near a local sandpit just outside of a small town in Alberta. *4* Later, the nearby Museum was called and archeologists looked and dug at the site. *5* The items were taken from the pit and moved to the Museum to look over closer. *6* It has been decided that the items will soon be placed out for people to see after they look it over so that people can enjoy the history of their great land.

7 After looking at the items for awhile, archeologists said that the items were a bunch of tools for cutting and scraping. *8* In addition, they found part of a shelter and a fire pit. *9* However, the stone used for the tools were not from this area and they think the items found were from people traveling long ago as the site had been used many times before its destruction. *10* It could also be an area for recreation, parties and even overnight camp outs and the Museum believes that the end of the area was caused by mud during a flood.

11 The sandpit is still closed to the public for the Museum to continue to dig the site in hopes of finding more pieces of human activity. *12* "For right now, we have only begun to find what items could be here and we will not lose sleep on this matter!" said an archeologist who works for the Museum. *13* For more information on recent items found, check out the Museum's Website at http://www.museum/artifacts.com/.

The Vocabulary Thing

Challenging students to find alternatives for the word *thing* represents a useful method to improve word choices in writing. The exercise will be most effective if you have noted overuse of *thing* in students' writing. If such is the case, you might create a supplementary exercise with examples selected from your students' work.

Each of the following exemplars includes the word *thing*. Ask students to identify alternative wording to add color to the writing. Students could employ sticky notes to complete the activity.

Many teachers emphasize the importance of connotative vocabulary through a related exercise titled "Said Is Dead." With your students, brainstorm synonyms for the word *said*. Examples include *demanded, uttered, stammered, proclaimed, whispered, declared*, and *expressed*. Ask students to locate examples of *said* in their writing, to determine whether more colorful synonyms are appropriate, and to suggest alternative words, where appropriate. Remember that *said* should not always be replaced, though. It may be the preferred choice for direct statements and is often the best choice in news stories. The word *said* need not always be dead!

After students do the exercise, have them work independently or with a partner to read through compositions to locate use of the word *thing* and to revise to improve the vocabulary.

Other words that students are often wise to replace include *awesome, great, big*, and *cool*. Students can be challenged to list such colorless, overused words.

EXEMPLAR A

(Essay about unfair treatment of young people)

Another big thing today is equality in age. You have to be so old to do this or to do that or to get a certain job. Having to be 18 to vote discriminates against young people. Most 16 year olds could decide about voting preferences. In addition, if a younger person competes with an older person for a job, guess who wins the competition?

EXEMPLAR B

(Story focused on finding a bottle on the seashore with a note in it)

She sat down and began writing down her name, address and other information. Then, taking her father's wine bottle, she stuck the note inside. She then walked to the beach and threw the bottle as far as she could and hoped that someone would go through the same thing.

EXEMPLAR C

(Essay about the challenges of working as a hotel manager)

I learned things that night. I grew in admiration for hotel managers and their jobs. They have to ensure that everything is working in every room, decide whether or not to hire someone, ensure that room-service is effective. They also have to worry about the hotel's reputation meaning that they regularly check websites to ensure that the property is five-star.

Colorful Choices

Many teachers believe that verbs, as well as other parts of speech, are best taught in the context of students' writing. You may wish to begin with a review of verbs—words that express action or being—as you remind students that thoughtfully chosen verbs add color and interest to writing. As Strunk and White write in *The Elements of Style*, Fourth Edition, "It is nouns and verbs, not their assistants, that give good writing its toughness and color."

Guide your students through a consideration of the student's choice of verbs in Exemplar A, "Ghosts." Students should identify the verbs and then note the most colorful ones, such as *crash-landed*, *froze*, *popped*, and *sped*. These colorful verbs help the reader in visualizing the events.

In Exemplar B, "Forever Mine," some verbs have been underlined. Ask students to identify the most colorful or connotative choice for each underlined pair and to suggest another possibility in the bracketed section after each underlined pair. Students may complete the activity individually or in small groups. If students employ a thesaurus to locate possibilities, remind them to ensure that their choice fits the context of the writing.

Follow the exercise by having students revise one of their own compositions to improve word choices.

As an extension activity, ask students to employ a passage from their own writing to create an exercise similar to that on the next page. Presented anonymously, the exercises can become valuable learning resources.

EXEMPLAR A

Ghosts

Boom! The large box, wrapped in brown paper and tied with string crash-landed on our driveway. I gazed out my window and froze with astonishment. How did the box arrive there? As I wondered, an idea popped into my head. I decided to call Louise to invite her to inspect the box with me and to inspect the contents with me. Before long, Louise sped up on her bicycle. "Louise, Louise, look!" I stammered.

Louise spied a piece of paper tied to the box. It read, "To the Finder of This Box: This box contains a tiny marble statue. We want to be rid of it because every night when it turns pitch black, the statue turns into a dangerous ghost."

EXEMPLAR B

Forever Mine

There was a strange box on the street. Laura was frightened. She walked/shuffled (   ) through the autumn leaves towards the box. Laura pulled/tugged (   ) at her skirt which had gotten caught on a twig. It was the year l995. She was waiting for her mother to rush/come (   ) outside to take her to school.

"Mom," Laura called/shouted (   ) with anxiety in her voice. "Come out here, please!" She moved/edged (   ) closer to the box. There was something scratching inside the box. Laura hoped it was a dog. She was awfully lonely. Everybody at school thought she was weird. Maybe she was. Laura did not know. Her mother burst/hurried (   ) through the door. Laura told her mother the story and they opened the crate.

Directions for Exemplar B:

1. For each underlined pair of verbs above, circle the word that brings most color to the writing.
2. In each space within brackets, insert a different verb that brings color to the writing. You may refer to a thesaurus, if desired.

Verb Challenge

Since most verbs are action words, the writer's appropriate choice of verbs paints the canvas so that readers can effortlessly and effectively visualize the text.

In the following exemplar, some verbs have been underlined. Challenge students to work independently or with a partner to identify more colorful alternatives. Some possibilities have been listed below:

Original Word	Replacement
walked	sauntered
take (a look)	steal
ran	raced
said	replied
ate	wolfed down
said	remarked
got	located
saw	noticed
helped	boosted
put	deposited
drove	motored
had	consumed

After the activity, engage students in revising one of their own compositions to enhance the vitality of verb choices.

Note that the featured exemplar, "Mysterious Box," has been used for another purpose in this book. A single exemplar can be employed for varied instructional purposes. Your decision about instructional use of any exemplar will be guided by needs that you assess in your students' writing. A single exemplar can usefully be employed with different students and different classes for different purposes.

Mysterious Box

I <u>walked</u> over to the big box. I was very curious about what was inside.

There was a little hole in the box, and I decided to take a peek. Unfortunately, it was too dark to <u>take a look</u>. The box was very, very big.

I <u>ran</u> to my mom and asked if I could open the box. My mom <u>said</u> maybe after lunch. It was lunchtime so I <u>ate</u> two hotdogs. After, I pulled the enormous, heavy box into my yard. My mom <u>said</u> I was strong. My mom <u>got</u> a screwdriver and we unscrewed all the bolts. I was excited to see what was inside with my mom. It was a box full of stacked one-hundred dollar bills. When my mom <u>saw</u> the cash she almost fainted. I <u>helped</u> her back to her feet. My mom and I were millionaires. My mom and I were very excited and happy.

The next day my Mom and I loaded all the money in the truck. My mom and I drove to the bank and <u>put</u> money in our savings account. My mom and I <u>drove</u> back to our house. My mom and I celebrated by watching a movie. We <u>had</u> lots of pop, popcorn and candy. My mom and I were very happy and never went bankrupt.

Direction:

Replace each underlined verb with a specific colorful verb.

walked _____	take a look _____
ran _____	said _____
ate _____	said _____
got _____	saw _____
helped _____	put _____
drove _____	had _____

Assessing Word Choice

After students have completed "Verb Challenge" (see pages 113–14), invite them do this activity, which uses the same text, "Mysterious Box." In this activity, students rate the vocabulary with a rubric and suggest improvements beyond the verb improvements already made.

Ask students to work individually or with a partner to score the original vocabulary in "Mysterious Box" with the rubric provided. Then, challenge students to suggest improvements to word choices beyond those they have already made and to note them. You might direct students to change the text to include direct speech set off in double quotation marks. Use of someone's exact words brightens vocabulary. Note the benefit of direct speech in the following revision to the "Mysterious Box" exemplar:

Original Text: I ran over to my mom and asked her if I could open the box. My mom said maybe after lunch.

Possible Revision: I ran over to my mom and pleaded, "Mom, may I please open the box?"

My mom replied, "Maybe after lunch."

Invite students to use the rubric to score their revised version of "Mysterious Box."

Extend the activity by having students use the rubric to score one of their own compositions for word choices. They can then make revisions focused on improved verb and other vocabulary choices, and note their new ratings on the rubric.

Mysterious Box

I walked over to the big box. I was very curious about what was inside.

There was a little hole in the box, and I decided to take a peek. Unfortunately, it was too dark to take a look. The box was very, very big.

I ran to my mom and asked if I could open the box. My mom said maybe after lunch. It was lunchtime so I ate two hotdogs. After, I pulled the enormous, heavy box into my yard. My mom said I was strong. My mom got a screwdriver and we unscrewed all the bolts. I was excited to see what was inside with my mom. It was a box full of stacked one-hundred dollar bills. When my mom saw the cash she almost fainted. I helped her back to her feet. My mom and I were millionaires. My mom and I were very excited and happy.

The next day my Mom and I loaded all the money in the truck. My mom and I drove to the bank and put our money in our savings account. My mom and I drove back to our house. My mom and I celebrated by watching a movie. We had lots of pop, popcorn and candy. My mom and I were very happy and never went bankrupt.

5	4	3	2	1
Words are consistently appropriate, effective, and purposefully selected.	Words are usually appropriate, effective, and purposefully selected.	Words are sometimes appropriate and effective, but tend to be general.	Words are often imprecise or redundant.	Words are often unclear, misused, and inaccurate.

To Be or Not to Be

Exemplars can be used to encourage choice of precise and colorful verbs. The following exemplars illustrate the value of sometimes seeking alternatives to forms of the verb *to be* in writing. Although *to be* is the most used verb in the English language and is appropriate in many instances, forms of the verb, such as *I am* and *I was*, can be overused. Students can add color to their writing by considering appropriate alternatives.

Sometimes, the verb *to be* is overused and weakly used because the writer employs passive rather than active voice. Voice in verbs refers to whether the subject is acting or is being acted upon. For instance: "Mary received the award" or "Mary receives the award" is written in active voice; however, "The award was received by Mary" or "The award is received by Mary" is written in passive voice. You might want to list examples of active and passive voice on the board and then challenge students to consider why many writers use the active voice as often as possible. Active voice is less wordy and makes writing livelier by focusing attention on the performer of the action rather than away from the performer of the action; overuse of passive voice results in dull writing.

Have students compare the two exemplars with a focus on the underlined verbs. Challenge students to choose the exemplar that has more colorful verbs (Exemplar B), and to place a star or checkmark above examples of passive voice, such as *was prevented*, *was shoved*, and *were lined up*. Stress that although forms of the verb *to be* and passive voice sometimes work best for a writer, alternatives often result in clearer, more memorable writing.

After work with the exemplars, have students review a composition of their own to note preferred alternatives to the verb *to be* and to use of the passive voice.

EXEMPLAR A

When I <u>was</u> out on the pool deck, the gleaming sun was so bright, I <u>was prevented</u> from noticing my surroundings. Before long I <u>was shoved</u> into the sparkling water that <u>was</u> very cold. When I <u>was</u> able to breathe easily again, I noticed the diving boards aligned from shortest to tallest. Divers <u>were lined up</u> by lifeguards behind the boards. The divers <u>were</u> happy to splash into the water.

EXEMPLAR B

When I <u>stumbled</u> out on the pool deck, the gleaming sun <u>blinded</u> me and prevented me from noticing my surroundings. Before long a prankster <u>shoved</u> me into the sparkling water, so cold that it spread gooseflesh throughout my body. When I <u>caught</u> my breath, I noticed the diving boards aligned from shortest to tallest. Lifeguards <u>lined</u> divers behind the boards. The divers <u>shrieked</u> as they splashed into the water.

Directions:

1. Identify the exemplar that has the most colorful verbs. _____

2. Explain the advantages of using these colorful verbs in writing. _____

   _____

3. Place a star or checkmark above three examples of passive voice in the exemplars above:

   _____   _____   _____

4. Explain the advantages of active rather than passive voice in the two exemplars.

   _____

   _____

Adding Rich Details

This activity, which could serve as a reinforcement exercise for work in word choices, combines several vocabulary activities, such as selecting effective words, assessing vocabulary, and replacing colorless verbs.

For Exemplar A, encourage students to underline effective words and then to rate them for vocabulary. Students might note the following effective word choices: *proclaimed, bopped, giggled, zoomed, yelled, vanished, fumed,* and *bellowed.* Discuss choices and ratings with the class.

Next, have students review Exemplar B, an alternative version of "A Trip to the Future." Students should substitute more effective word choices for the underlined words. Possible improvements to Exemplar B have been charted below:

Original	Possible Replacements
made	constructed
got into	boarded
gave us	handed over
came back	returned
bad old	wicked
took	stole

Students may find it interesting to consider that sometimes simple, plain words are most effective. For example, *found* is likely stronger than *located* and *trying* is likely better than *attempting*.

After the activities, students should revise one of their own compositions to improve word choices.

Note: "A Trip to the Future" also lends itself especially well to the study of dialogue and how to handle it. If you decide to use Exemplar A that way, remember that every time the speaker changes, a new paragraph should begin.

EXEMPLAR A

A Trip to the Future

"There! I'm done!" I proclaimed. "The number one, the best, the most awesome time machine on earth!" I hopped into my time machine, which was made out of an old cardboard box.

"Come on Cadet!" I yelled, "Strap on your time goggles!" Cadet, who is my teddy bear, has pink goggles with flowers on them. Mine are blue. I giggled as we zoomed into hyperspace. I decided to type in let's see ... 2054. Earrrrchh! We were in 2054. "Cool! Look at those Rockets! They're zooming all over the place!" I yelled. I parked the time machine and we got into a rocket. "You have to be over three years old to drive a rocket," announced the robot, which was beside me. I told him I was seven and he gave us the keys, and we were off. After we came back, the time machine was gone! The robot had vanished too.

"Oh that bad old robot!" I fumed. "He took our time machine!!" We followed the trail of oil, which the robot had left behind. It led all the way to the secret lab. We found the robot trying to make the time machine work.

"Ha-ha! We have you now, Mr. Robot!!" I bellowed.

Directions:

1. Underline all of the effective verbs.
2. Use the rubric to score this piece for word choice.

Rubric for Scoring Word Choice

5	4	3	2	1
Words are consistently appropriate, effective, and purposefully selected.	Words are usually appropriate, effective, and purposefully selected.	Words are sometimes appropriate and effective, but tend to be general.	Words are often imprecise or redundant.	Words are often unclear, misused, and inaccurate.

EXEMPLAR B

A Trip to the Future

"There! I'm done!" I proclaimed. "The number one, the best, the most awesome time machine on earth!" I hopped into my time machine, which was <u>made</u> out of an old cardboard box.

"Come on Cadet!" I yelled, "Strap on your time goggles!" Cadet, who is my teddy bear, has pink goggles with flowers on them. Mine are blue. I giggled as we zoomed into hyperspace. I decided to type in let's see ... 2054. Earrrrrchh! We were in 2054. "Cool! <u>Look</u> at those Rockets! They're zooming all over the place!" I yelled. I parked the time machine and we <u>got into</u> a rocket. "You have to be over three years old to drive a rocket," announced the robot, which was beside me. I told him I was seven and he <u>gave us</u> the keys, and we were off. After we <u>came back</u>, the time machine was gone! The robot had <u>vanished</u> too.

"Oh that <u>bad old</u> robot!" I fumed. "He <u>took</u> our time machine!!" We followed the trail of oil, which the robot had left behind. It led all the way to the secret lab. We <u>found</u> the robot <u>trying</u> to make the time machine work.

"Ha-ha! We have you now, Mr. Robot!!" I bellowed.

Directions:

1. Reread the piece of work above, noting the underlined words.
2. Replace the underlined words with more effective words.

Choices in Context

This activity illustrates how cloze can be employed to challenge students to think about their choices as writers. Cloze is an instructional technique in which selected words or chunks of text are deleted from a passage. In its attention to adjectives, the exemplar work also illustrates teaching grammar in the context of students' writing.

The teacher who created the activity reminded students that original figures of speech, well-chosen adjectives, and appropriate detail add richness and voice to a story. Following their work with the cloze exercise, students read the complete text to determine whether their choices were as effective as the original author's choices. In the discussion, the teacher emphasized that writers consciously make choices.

Once your students complete work with the exemplars, have them revise one of their own stories. They should add at least one original figure of speech, add at least one effective adjective, add at least three original relevant details, and strengthen the conclusion with a reaction, realization, or surprising twist.

As illustrated in this activity, when working with exemplars to create learning resources, teachers often focus on four or five aspects of writing. Such resources work especially well with students who are already familiar with the aspects selected. For example, students who worked with this exemplar already knew about similes, adjectives, adverbs, details that show, and effective endings.

Larry's Surprise

Larry hit his snooze alarm for the fourth time that morning. When his alarm went off again, he jumped out of bed realizing that even if he got up at that moment, he would still be rushed getting dressed and packing his lunch for school. He raced down the hallway nearly tripping as he struggled to pull his shirt over his head.

When he arrived at school with his lunchbox, he felt as hungry as *1* _____

_____.

He hadn't eaten breakfast. The morning seemed to drag, and finally the bell rang.

It was lunch time! Larry grabbed his lunchbox from his locker and sprinted down

the *2* _____ hallway to the

3 _____ lunchroom. He opened his lunchbox

quickly. He couldn't believe what he saw.

4 _____ !

_____ ! _____ !

There was a mouse peeking out of his lunchbox, and it ate Larry's sandwich! He told himself from then on *5* _____

_____

Directions:

1. Add an interesting simile.
2. Add an adjective.
3. Add an adjective.
4. How did Larry react to seeing a mouse in his lunchbox? Add three interesting, relevant details.
5. Add an interesting and appropriate reaction or realization.

Larry's Surprise

Larry hit his snooze alarm for the fourth time that morning. When his alarm went off again, he jumped out of bed realizing that even if he got up at that moment, he would still be rushed getting dressed and packing his lunch for school. He raced down the hallway nearly tripping as he struggled to pull his shirt over his head.

When he arrived at school with his lunchbox, he felt as hungry as a bear who just awoke from hibernation. He hadn't eaten breakfast. The morning seemed to drag, and finally the bell rang. It was lunch time! Larry grabbed his lunchbox from his locker and sprinted down the crowded hallway to the noisy lunchroom. He opened his lunchbox quickly. He couldn't believe what he saw. His eyes popped out! He yelled! He nearly fell off his chair! There was a mouse peeking out of his lunchbox, and it ate Larry's sandwich! He told himself from then on, he'd better wake up earlier and double-check his lunch before leaving the house to go to school!

Playful Exemplar Activity — From Descriptive to Dull

Connotative vocabulary is rich in suggested meaning beyond the literal or basic meaning. For example, a suitor may describe his loved one as being like a rose, but would be unwise to compare her to a dandelion or a stinkweed. By rewriting text that has connotative vocabulary into text with colorless vocabulary, students learn the importance of words that help the reader clearly visualize and comprehend the text.

Decide whether you would like students to work on their own or in small groups. After providing students with copies of the exemplar on the next page, have them change five words so that descriptive vocabulary becomes dull and ordinary. Students may rewrite the sentences to change the vocabulary. Perhaps you could have them mark changes on an overhead transparency of the text so that classmates can read the degraded vocabulary in context. One member of each group should read the "revised" version of the text, which might sound something like this:

> The elevator doors opened and I ran into my office. I listened for the phone to ring. I was expecting a call to the board room by my mean boss. I was upset—no call. I assured myself that Mr. Perfect would be okay with me being late and allow me the chance to pay him back for losing the annual report. This was but a slight delay. The boss hurried into the room.

Perhaps offer a small prize to the student or group whose vocabulary changes do the most damage to the piece.

Conclude by having students revise one of their own compositions to improve word choices.

EXEMPLAR

When the elevator doors finally opened I tore into my office. My ears strained for the sound of the clanging phone. I was expecting a summons to the board room by my cantankerous boss. I stood stiffly and awkwardly—no call. I assured myself that Mr. Perfect would forgive my being late and allow me the opportunity to compensate for having misplaced the annual report. This was but a momentary reprieve. Mr. Perfect burst through the door!

Directions:

Review the exemplar above and replace five vivid, concrete words with dull, colorless words. You may recast sentences.

Vivid words: _____

Dull words: _____

Playful Exemplar:

_____

_____

_____

_____

_____

_____

_____

_____

6. Voice

Writing with voice is characterized by an appropriate tone, by evidence of honesty and caring about one's writing, and by originality in expression. This chapter of exemplar-based lessons helps students transfer their learning about voice into a sense of unique voice in their own writing.

- **Honest, Original Expression** shows students writing characterized by originality and writing ridden with clichés, and challenges them to recognize the strengths of the former.
- **Original Imagery** reminds students of the power of fresh imagery, including figures of speech, in their writing.
- **First-Person Writing and Dialogue** nudges students to reflect on choices that will help them project a clear, appropriate voice in writing.
- **Intensifying Voice** combines analysis of several aspects of voice: caring, originality, and tone.
- **Imaginative Detail and Use of Devices** focuses on how originality of detail combines with devices, such as humor and figurative language, to create voice in writing.

Writing experts emphasize these important characteristics of voice:

- honesty and evidence of caring about one's writing rather than wooden and contrived writing
- originality in word choice and choice of detail rather than familiar detail and clichés

Although clichés, such as "a bump on a log," once had originality, they have lost their power through overuse. Clichés are the enemy of voice in writing! Be wary, too, of vague expressions, such as "or anything," which appears in Exemplar B—they are weak filler and do not add genuine detail.

The following sets of short poems illustrate voice. Have students read Exemplars A and B as a set and then Exemplars C and D as a set to determine which version demonstrates a stronger voice. Prompt them to identify language and details that are more original. Is one version more honest and caring than the other?

Exemplar A, "My Father's Old Sweater," contains nine original word choices, such as *combat*, and detail, such as Autumn chill. The detail about arms of love is more original than the point in Exemplar B about the father being with the author still. Exemplar A also reflects that greater care was taken because Exemplar B's "or anything" is a rather vague phrase that adds nothing to the idea of being cold. In Exemplar C, cool as a cucumber is a cliché. Proudly cool in the shade, which appears in Exemplar D, is more original.

After this individual or small-group activity, have students revise a piece of their own writing to add originality in word choice and detail.

As an extension activity, have students work in groups to list clichés on chart paper and then to share with classmates. One class generated lists that included the following clichés:

- to get cold feet
- a can of worms
- like a chicken with its head cut off
- not my cup of tea

EXEMPLAR A

My Father's Old Sweater

I wore his sweater for hours last night
not to combat the Autumn chill
But imagining again that arms of love
were round about me and with me still.

EXEMPLAR B

My Father's Old Sweater

I wore his sweater for hours last night
Not because I was cold or anything
But to remind me of my father
Who died but is with me still.

EXEMPLAR C

A patch of green
in my flower bed
the fern grows
in a world of its own
cool as a cucumber in the shade
of my garden waterfall.
I understand them well.
They keep their distance
and I keep mine.

EXEMPLAR D

Like green lace
edging a fringe of scarlet lilies
the fern grows
wary of the touch
proudly cool in the shade
of my garden waterfall.
I understand their distance,
and I keep mine.

Original Imagery

In this variation on the activity of challenging students to choose original imagery, students identify from two or three exemplars the strongest original imagery: imagery that lends voice to the writing. Their focus is figures of speech.

The following three exemplars are excerpts from students' stories. Ask students to identify the simile in each exemplar and then identify the metaphor or simile that is most original.

The preferred version is Exemplar A since *as sharp as knives* (Exemplar B) and references to eagle eyes (Exemplar C) are more familiar. *Like a crane picking up debris from a demolition site* is most original.

After work with the activity, prompt students to revise any of their own compositions that would benefit from original metaphors or similes to create voice. Some students benefit from work with a partner to complete the revision activity. The addition of even one original comparison frequently yields impressive benefit to the text. Rubric scores for content and word choice improve.

Remind students that while figures of speech should be original, they should also be familiar to the audience. Writers demonstrate voice when they select familiar detail that is original in the comparison.

EXEMPLAR A

I looked in the huge box another time to determine if anything remained inside. Sure enough, tucked away in a corner were four deflated volleyballs with four air pumps. I just had to call my friend, Frank. Speechless, Frank rushed to my home. His mouth dropped open like a crane picking up debris from a demolition side.

EXEMPLAR B

A few days later, I heard a weird sound snort. Since it was something I'd never experienced before, my first reaction moved me to check the box. As soon as I opened the flaps, a baby tyrannosaurus squirmed out. It had orange eyes, red-green skin and teeth as sharp as knives.

EXEMPLAR C

Right after school we dashed to check the hidden trunk. Bad luck was with us. The lid wouldn't budge. Yet there wasn't a keyhole. It would require someone with eagle eyes to see it.

First-Person Writing and Dialogue

Caring about one's writing is a critical feature of voice in writing. It is demonstrated by conveying honest emotions, such as outrage, passion, joy, anger, or empathy. Honesty and caring are evident through the following features:

- personal accounts written in the first person, using *I*
- dialogue that illustrates emotional responses:
  "I don't believe this is happening to us," I whispered to Charley.
  "Be patient," he answered calmly.

The following pair of exemplars can be used as a teaching tool to connect first-person writing and emotional response through dialogue to writing with voice. Ask students to compare Exemplars A and B. How does Exemplar B, the original student piece, convey voice, which is missing in Exemplar A? Students should note the advantages of the first-person account and of the dialogue to convey emotion effectively. Be sure to point out that dialogue is effective when it suits the words and speech patterns of the individual speakers. The exact natural-sounding words, placed within double quotation marks, will include contractions, short sentences, and sentence fragments. Every time the speaker changes, a new paragraph should begin. Students may also find it interesting to realize that the kind of language appropriate in dialogue—for example, *stinks*—is likely inappropriate for indirect speech.

After they have completed the activity, have students review a composition written in the first person to strengthen honest, emotional responses. Alternatively, they could rewrite a section of a text written in third person (omniscient author) in first person, putting an emphasis on honest, emotional responses.

Teachers who work with reluctant writers have often pointed out that many students are more fluent with first-person narratives than with omniscient author narratives. First-person writing reminds these students to dip into the well of their own experiences when they write. It also gives students permission to use familiar language.

EXEMPLAR A

As he glanced out of the muddy window of his jeep, he looked at his new residence —the Sunshine State apartment. As he stepped out of the blue vehicle his mother blurted that this will be a wonderful change. Austin sighed in agreement but he knew he would miss his friends. His mother suggested that they go in. He muttered to himself that the place stunk.

EXEMPLAR B

Glancing out of the muddy window of the jeep, I looked up into the eyes of my new Sunshine State apartment. As I stepped out of the blue vehicle, my mother blurted, "Oh, Austin, won't this be a wonderful change?"

"Sure, I guess," I sighed, missing my friends.

"Come on; let's go in!" my mother smiled as she headed for the doors.

"This stinks," I muttered to myself as I followed her.

Intensifying Voice

Each of the next three exemplars features questions to focus students on recognizing voice in writing. Students may work individually or in small groups to complete the assignment. You may choose to have students work together on two of the exemplars and to work independently on one that you would assess. Plan to have students share group-work responses in full-class discussion.

After they finish work with the exemplars, prompt students to identify something they feel strongly about and to give it some thought. Their topic might be

- a place in the world that is important to them
- a person who has made a difference
- something funny that has happened to them
- a situation that has concerned them

Challenge students to write about the topic of their choice in the first person. Developing compositions of one or two paragraphs would be fine. Later, when they are in the revision stage, encourage them to check for evidence of caring about the topic, original word choice, original details, and original imagery, including figures of speech. In your assessment of the writing, be sure to emphasize these features of voice rather than any errors with conventions.

Other ways to have students discover and intensify voice in writing include dramatization and pre-writing exercises focused on emotions.

For dramatization, use a text that features a conflict or dramatic action between two or more characters. As students dramatize the text, they focus on capturing the voices of the characters they are portraying.

Pre-writing exercises focused on emotions help students consider feelings related to important places, persons, funny events, and situations of concern. One way to do this is to invite students to separate thoughts and feelings on the topic of choice. One possible structure is shown below.

A Place in the World That Is Important to Me

Ideas and Details About Why It is Important	Feelings Related to the Place

A Box of Surprises

After I found the large turtle, I immediately thought about how to <u>care</u> for it. Since I knew turtle lived in saltwater, I half carried, half dragged the turtle into our swimming pool and dumped in all of my mom's baking salt. The turtle looked extremely happy to be in the water, but it had a bored expression too. I decided to buy some lily pads from the pet store down the road. But right now, I decided to get on my swimsuit and swim with the turtle. When I got in the water, the turtle kept on touching me and then swimming away. I had two opinions on that. One, it wanted to play tag. Or two, it was figuring out what I was. I decided on one and swam after it. We were soon very tired and I went to get two inflatable beach chairs (one for me, the other for the turtle) so we could relax in the water. Taking <u>care</u> of animals is much harder that it looks. A few days later, the turtle looked as if it was hungry. I went to my computer and found out that turtles like to eat leaves, grass and jelly. So I went back outside and grabbed as much grass as I could and dropped it in the pool.

"It would be nice if he could get his own food," I grumbled.

I dumped in some leaves from my leaf pile and went inside to get some grape jelly. I grabbed the jar and then dumped it in the swimming pool. The turtle's favorite food in my opinion is jelly.

Directions:

1. How does the writer demonstrate caring about the topic?
2. Identify two original details and two carefully chosen words that add voice to the piece.
3. Find two places in this exemplar where you could insert asides—comments to the reader, set in brackets—to add humor.

EXEMPLAR B

Danielle was pulled awake by her little sister Carrie.

"I heard a sound," she whispered loudly.

Danielle stumbled out of bed and sleepily rubbed her eyes.

"What did you say?" whispered Danielle.

"I said I heard something."

"What sort of noise?"

Carrie didn't answer. Carrie wasn't there. Danielle turned cold. She felt like something was watching her. She was scared.

Where had Carrie disappeared to? Where had she gone?

Danielle slipped out of bed. She didn't know where she was going to go, but it didn't matter.

Carrie had to be somewhere that was for sure. She crept down the hall and peeked in her parents' room. They were fast asleep. She then peeked in her sister's room. Carrie wasn't there but something else was in plain view—a book, an old book. She advanced into the room.

Directions:

1. How does the writer demonstrate caring about the topic?
2. Add or change two words to intensify the voice.
3. Add two original details to intensify the voice.

EXEMPLAR C

Debate was my life. Since I had been a small child I had been able to argue my way out of anything. I had even been told I could convince someone that sky was green and the grass was blue.

I had been in debate club since I was in Grade Seven. Each day, my debating buddies and I would meet in the Art Room for forty-five minutes and hold impromptu debates. We would set up the tables and argue over nothing for the next half hour.

Truly, these were the best days I'd experienced.

One day, after English, my friend Jake and I met up on our way to the Art Room.

"Hey Miles!" he said as he ran up beside me. "Ready to lose another one?"

"Hah! You couldn't beat me even if you tried," I laughed.

We kept up the discussion about who could out-debate whom until we reached the Art Room.

Directions:

1. How does the writer demonstrate caring about the topic?
2. Underline the parts of the story that show the author's voice.

Imaginative Detail and Use of Devices

Often, teachers discover that they have one or more students who can be described as gifted writers for their particular age or grade. Their abilities as writers may include many of the following characteristics:

- imaginative choice of detail
- superior command of language
- sophisticated use of devices, such as humor, exaggeration, sarcasm, irony, and figurative language
- strong voice
- meticulous research and planning

Use the exemplar "The Perfect Pet," written by a student at the beginning of Grade 4, to have students identify examples of

- humor (e.g. "I was relieved that I didn't have to sit so long.")
- detail that shows imagination (e.g., the notion that a kitten would magically hatch from an egg)
- sarcasm (e.g., "Now I see what was meant by big mouth.")
- voice that shows an emotional reaction (e.g., "Eeep! I thought, "Mr. Accessories.")

Challenge students to identify two effective sentences and to explain their choices. Possibilities include these:

- "Soon the egg was too big for my room!" (an exclamatory sentence that adds variety and interest)
- "As quick as a lightning bolt, as the book had promised, a tiny yellow egg appeared on my finely quilted bed." (a sentence that begins with something other than the subject that adds variety to sentence patterns)

Have students review a composition of their own and use sticky notes to mark examples of effective techniques. Challenge students to revise their own work to include at least one example of a technique that would enhance their compositions.

EXEMPLAR

The Perfect Pet

"Aha! I cried. I have found *The Magic Pet* book.
I searched through the chapter entitled "Egg Pets."
Intelligent Duck? Nope.
Rancid Rat? No, too smelly.
OUTSTANDING KITTEN? Yes!
I read the instructions:

> Say: Mjuta libber kitten and a tiny yellow egg will appear. Everyday when the moon is full, sit on the egg until midnight. The egg will grow to its maximum size of 30 meters tall and 20 meters wide. When it reaches its maximum you will not sit on the egg anymore. Five days later it will hatch and out comes an intelligent kitten.

Then in small print it said, "Beware of its big mouth."
Big mouth; big deal! I shouted, "Mjuta libber, Kitten!"
As quick as a lightning bolt as the book promised, a tiny yellow egg appeared on my finely quilted bed. The moon was full. With hope I climbed on the bed and sat on the egg.
Right away magic did its work. The egg started to grow and grow and GROW! Boy was I really unprepared. That night I put a spell on myself so I wouldn't be sleepy. I grabbed my book and mounted the egg. The egg started to grow. Soon the egg was too big for my room! So I cast a spell so my room would grow as the egg grew. In only three days the egg grew to its maximum size of 30 meters tall and 20 meters wide. I was relieved that I didn't have to sit so long. The egg was huge and I was puny.
Five days later as predicted the egg hatched neatly. I dashed to the bed and the egg. Sure enough a tiny adorable kitten that fit on my hand came out.
"Hi!" the kitten greeted me warmly. It was a wonder that the kitten had come out of such a gigantic egg. I asked the kitten why.
He explained, "I need a lot of room for my books, bathtub, sink, etc., etc.!"
"Eeep!" I thought, "Mr. Accessories."
"For your information I don't think I like you," he exclaimed as if he had read my mind.
Now I see what was meant by big mouth!
"Big mouth, GIANT deal! Now I'll just park the egg in that empty corner," he pointed.
That all happened a month ago. Now we decided the egg was big enough for two, so we moved into the egg, sold our house and moved to a cozy corner in Thousand Acre Woods. The only thing is that the egg is getting BIGGER AND BIGGER!
I'm cooking up a potion. The kitten just came up. Now he is getting bigger!
"Did you drink the potion? Did you? Did you?"
No answer.

7. Conventions

Conventional mechanics—punctuation, spelling, and capitalization—and conventional usage (such matters as sentence completeness and subject–verb agreement) are frequently required in writing. An exception would be when an author dramatizes the unconventional usage of a region or group. This section illustrates possibilities for employing exemplars so that students learn conventional mechanics and usage.

- **Learning Parts of Speech** employs exemplars so that students learn grammatical terminology in context.
- **Standard Usage Mini-Lessons** presents an instructional strategy for use of students' writing for teaching and learning about conventions.
- **Dictation Exercises to Learn Conventions** illustrates a powerful instructional strategy that employs exemplars for students to learn conventions.
- **Editing Codes** engages students in use of editing symbols to assess writing.

Learning Parts of Speech

Exemplars powerfully teach parts of speech within the context of a complete written text. This context allows students to learn that adjectives, adverbs, and other parts of speech are more than just labels. Exemplars invite students to consider the parts of speech that work best in context.

The next three exemplars illustrate possibilities for teaching and learning about adjectives, adverbs, and verbs. In each case, students are invited to suggest possibilities that work effectively in the composition. The object is not to match the author's choices in the exemplar; rather, it is to suggest possibilities as students learn about adjectives, adverbs, and verbs. Students often suggest better choices than the writer's choice. In Exemplar A, the writer employed the following adjectives: (1) moisture-deprived; (2) dilapidated; (3) dead; (4) aching. In Exemplar B, the writer chose the following adverbs: (1) definitely; (2) strongly; (3) personally; (4) heartily. In Exemplar C, the writer chose the following verbs: (1) rested; (2) chirped; (3) charmed; (4) pondered.

These exemplars reflect the use of cloze procedure. The procedure is especially beneficial to students who do not adequately focus on textual detail when they are reading or when they are revising their writing. The challenge to consider possibilities and to compare these to the author's choices encourages reflection based on close attention to text.

As a follow-up to these cloze exercises, challenge students to review a composition to identify and improve on the choice of adjectives, adverbs, and verbs. Most students would work most effectively if they read their compositions three times—first, with a focus on adjectives, then on adverbs, and finally on verbs.

Adjectives: On My Bike

The *1* _____ fall air evaporated the perspiration on my wind-swept face as I raced headlong down the dusty gravel path. Despite the

2 _____ condition of the bike on which I saw, I still hugged corners like a hovercraft skimming the breakers with a rush of adrenaline, a rush that could be provided by few other activities. As the *3* _____ leaves became even deader with a crunch, crinkle, snap, I rocketed further down the twisted abyss of speed and motion; my overworked heart pulsated more laboriously. An unavoidable weariness began to hang over me like a dark storm cloud, heavy with thunder. My *4* _____ hamstrings and overheated body were not what they were five minutes ago … had it been five minutes? It seemed like centuries. So I hopped off my bike, and wondered why I had been compelled to go on in the first place.

EXEMPLAR B

Adverbs

<u>Anne Frank: The Diary of a Young Girl</u> 1_____ sits at the top of my

stack of favorite books. Even though Anne wrote the diary in the 1940s, it still

 2_____ appeals to teenagers today. I 3_____

relate to Anne's fears, dreams, goals and pet peeves. Many young people experience

similar thoughts and feelings as they grown up. I 4_____

recommend the book to my classmates.

EXEMPLAR C

Verbs

One graceful, quiet morning in Elfi Jaslin, a beautiful elf green with blond locks

relaxed in the hot blazing sun. As she 1_____ comfortably, animals

presented gifts to her. Birds 2_____ in the trees as flowers

3_____ the air with sweet aroma. Even though she had power over

nature, Jaslin treated creatures and plants with love and care. Happily she

4_____ her wonderful opportunities for later in the day.

Standard Usage Mini-Lessons

Exemplars can effectively teach matters of usage through mini-lessons. When assessing student work, use a checkmark or a highlighter to mark usage problems that you wish to feature in a mini-lesson. Have a volunteer copy the marked items on an overhead transparency for your use with students.

The following page illustrates a teacher's concern about improper use of the apostrophe, especially with plurals. The examples come from student work in the class. Provide your students with copies of the page and ask them to make corrections.

1. With our water we toasted the manager's health. (possessive)
2. A bad mark in school is a concern for parents. (plural)
3. Rockets on its boots appeared and he jetted right in front of me. (possessive)
4. Your mom suffered serious injuries in the accident. (plural)
5. I watched the phone drop as my eyes swelled with tears. (plural)
6. Let's see what happens. (contraction)
7. Dogs and cats were not allowed in the building. (plurals)
8. The Joneses live next door. (plural—or say the "Jones family lives")
9. Why don't I tell you the story? (contraction)
10. I have drivers' education class today. (plural)

After individual work, prompt students to confer with partners to confirm correct choices. Then, invite them to work independently or with a partner to edit for correct use of the apostrophe—or whatever aspect of standard usage is being targeted—in their own writing.

Correct Use of the Apostrophe

Step One: In these authentic examples of student writing, correct improper use of the apostrophe.

Step Two: With a partner, review samples of your own writing for correct apostrophe use. Identify up to five examples of improper use.

1. With our water we toasted the managers health.

_____

2. A bad mark in school is a large concern for parents'.

_____

3. Rockets on it's boots appeared and he jetted right in front of me.

_____

4. Your mom suffered serious injury's in the accident.

_____

5. I watched the phone drop as my eye's swelled with tears.

_____

6. Lets see what happens.

_____

7. Dog's and cat's were not allowed in the building.

_____

8. The Jone's live next door.

_____

9. Why dont I tell you the story?

_____

10. I have drivers education class today.

_____

Dictation Exercises to Learn Conventions

Dictation work represents a long-established instructional technique for students to learn conventional usage. As teachers slowly read a brief text, students write the text with an emphasis on correct usage. After the second reading of the text at a faster pace, students compare their work to the print version of the text, noting incorrect spelling and unconventional usage. The goal, of course, is for students to learn conventional usage.

Why not employ exemplars instead of "professional writing" for dictation exercises? Use of exemplars implicitly suggests the quality of work expected by the teacher. A caution is warranted, however: most school districts are governed by privacy laws. Be sure to have parental permission to use students' samples for dictation. Always remember to present the exemplars anonymously.

In selecting an exemplar for a dictation exercise, choose work that relates to usage you wish to emphasize. The following exemplars, selected from a single composition, would work well in a dictation exercise focused on changing paragraphs when speakers change. Teachers would expect improved work on the second dictation based on student learning from the first.

After dictation work, have students edit a section of their own writing to improve conventional usage related to the dictation.

EXEMPLAR A

The building walls gleamed in the scorching morning rays. My mother reached up and pressed the buzzer. "Hi!" she spoke into the intercom. "This is Claire Blake. I'm here to pick up my keys and move in!"

"I'll come down," the voice boomed. Slowly the door opened and a well-dressed man appeared. "Come on in!" he gestured. We proceeded in and shivered as the sun was blocked by the roof. He announced, "My name is Mr. Morton, follow me this way." We were led up to our suite. Being polite, Mr. Morton questioned, "How old are you young man?"

Timidly I whispered, "I'm Austin and I'm ten."

"Nice to meet you," Mr. Morton commented.

EXEMPLAR B

School, surprisingly, went by like a racecar. "Am I allowed to go to a pool party tonight?" I asked my mother. I then grabbed my swim trunks while waiting for an answer.

"Of course you can, if you're meeting new people!" she excitedly replied.

Sprinting down the street, my heart booming and smile gleaming, I reached the house. I breathed calmly then rang the doorbell.

"Hey, you're the new kid and I'm Jason!" spoke the boy in a welcoming tome.

"My name is Austin, actually," I corrected.

"Well Austin Actually, come on in!" As soon as I stepped in, I noticed a swimming pool and gasped, "Can we go swimming?"

"Of course you can," he smirked, "but you have to go off the diving board!" Swiftly putting on my swim suit, I put one foot in front of the other until I reached the pool side and looked up at the 20 foot diving board.

Editing Codes

Exemplars of student writing are logical resources for students to learn about editing codes. Before working with the next two exemplars, review differences between revision and editing:

- Revision is re-vision—taking another look at the writing to check for important features and to make helpful changes to the content, organization, sentence structure, word choice, and voice of the writing. In revision, writers become their own readers. They can make structural and content changes by applying specific criteria. They need to be aware that rewriting is likely necessary if writing is to be effective.
- Editing, as it is understood in a school context, involves correcting spelling, punctuation, capitalization, and usage in the writing. The focus is on conventions as a way to communicate with an audience.

Even though student writing may be weak in many areas, teachers are wise to encourage students to work with no more than four or five specific revision or editing criteria. Emphasize criteria related to demonstrated need in students' writing: with both revision and editing criteria, individual students may be working with different criteria on a given assignment. Challenging students to discover the method that works best for them in revising and editing is a good idea. Some students prefer sticky notes to mark changes; others prefer highlighters with different colors representing different criteria.

The assignment that involves the next two exemplars incorporates editing codes devised by a teacher—you might post the list on the chalkboard or on chart paper. The two questions to be answered about each exemplar remind students of the differences between editing and revision.

Editing Codes	
^	insert a word, letter, or phrase
sp	check spelling
/	delete
np	new paragraph
t	transpose
©	capitalize
	add a period

Determine whether you would like to have students work as a large group or in partners. Invite students to edit Exemplars A and B using the editing codes above. Alternatively, you and your students could use an exemplar to jointly develop editing codes. In that case, you would engage students in discussion about appropriate content and symbols.

Chester

One hot, summer day, I was playing outside with my two cousins. We are playing with my new puppy. Well, let's go to the beginning. One day, I was sitting on the steps on the steps, when suddenly a ginormous truck appeared in front of my eyes. I ran up to the sidewalk to see if it had left anything. Guess what, it had!!! It had left a box.

I went inside and brought the box along with me. Then I opened the box and in front of my eyes was the most adorably ever. I hadn't remembered ever wanting this dog. Now that I had it I don't understand why I wouldn't want it.

EXEMPLAR B

Lost Surfers

Ahla im Jade and im Nolise. We are ten year old girls. We are the youngest competing girl surfers in sunny Mexico. Today we are at the beach with our family. We are practicing for the competion on Friday.

While we were surfing we didn't notice our family was leaving without us When we stoped surfing we shrieked so loud out throats hert we starting looking all over the beach for them. So we searched all over Mexico. We looked at the icecream shop the shoe store and many other places.

The Nolise remembered that she had a Mexican guarter so she could call mom on her cellphone. We bolted to the telephone booth and called Mom. She was so joyfull that she ran to the beach and brought us back to the hotel safe and sound. The rest of the week was goo, we won and didnt get lost anymore. See you later toodleloo.

Directions:

1. Using the agreed-upon editing codes, edit each exemplar for spelling, punctuation, grammar, and capitalization.
2. What could be done to the content, organization, word choice, or sentence structure to make each piece more effective? Revise both pieces of work, making additions and deletions to the content, as necessary.
3. In a notebook, copy your versions. Share with a partner or with your class.

Self-Assessment of Writing

Title of Composition: _____

	Strengths	Areas for Improvement
Content		
Organization		
Sentence Structure		
Word Choice		
Voice		
Conventions		

How the Pros Do It

I have this question about my own writing:

Below I have listed two or three texts that may help me answer my question.	Below I have written how the texts answer my questions; there may also be an excerpt that helps me answer my question.

Reconsidering Interpretations

Title: _____

After my first reading, possibly the first part, chapter, or section, I thought that …

_____

_____

_____

_____

Is my understanding as complete and accurate as possible?
As I went on reading, I came to understand …

_____

_____

_____

_____

After carefully rereading text, especially checking sections I wondered about, I now understand that …

_____

_____

_____

_____

After discussing my understanding with others, I now think that …

_____

_____

_____

_____

Pre-Writing for Exposition

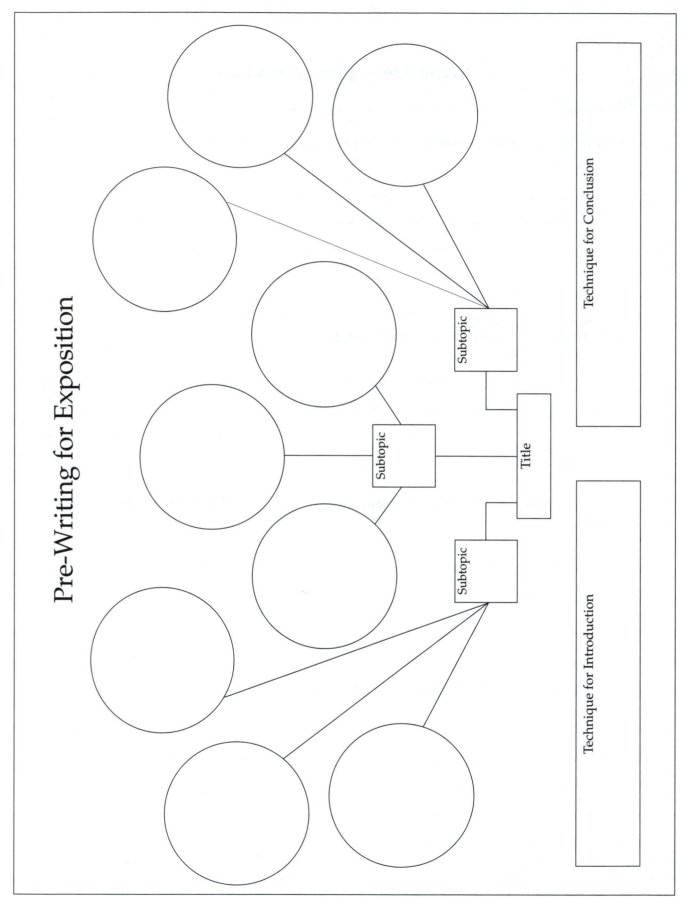

Title

Subtopic

Subtopic

Subtopic

Technique for Conclusion

Technique for Introduction

Index

Adjectives, 122, 141, 142
Adverbs, 141, 143
Apostrophe, 22, 144, 145
Audience, 15, 36

B.P.D.O.G. approach, 33, 62, 63
  Business letter planning form, 63
Business letters, 33
  Pre-writing, 62–65

Clichés, 128
Cloze, 104, 122, 141
Comparison and contrast, 70
Complex sentences, 85–86
  Creating, 85
Content, 6, 7, 15, 16, 36–60
  Choices, 122
  Effective and ineffective topic sentences, 36,
    52–54
  Engaging story beginnings and endings, 36,
    43-47
  Expository texts, 36, 50–51
  Off-topic sentence insertions, 36, 59–60
  Relevant and irrelevant detail (informational
    text), 36, 37–38
  Relevant and irrelevant detail (narrative text),
    36, 39–40
  Showing, not telling, 36, 55–56
  Strong endings for narrative texts, 36, 48–49
  Titles that work, 36, 57–58
  Writing variables for focus and inspiration, 36,
    41–42
Conventions, 6, 7, 15, 16, 140–49
  Dictation exercises to learn, 140, 146–47
  Editing codes, 140, 148–49
  Learning parts of speech, 140, 141–43
  Standard usage, 140, 144–45
Cooperative story writing, 80

Dialogue, 55, 132
Dictation, 146
Drafting, 20
Dramatization, 134

Editing, 22, 148
Editing codes, 148
Effective planning strategies, 14, 33–35
Effective writing
  Characteristics/Traits, 6, 7, 13, 15
  Content, 36
  Internalizing qualities of, 9
  Organization, 61
  Sentence variety, 84
  Strategies, 20
  Using exemplars to identify strategies, 20
  Word choice, 103
Exemplars
  A Box of Surprises, 135
  A Fish Story, 24, 25, 26
  A Profession Without Equal, 10, 80, 81
  A Trip to the Future, 10, 119, 120, 121
  Adjectives: On My Bike, 142
  Adverbs, 143
  Alternatives to "to be", 118
  Authors, 9
  Blizzard, 46
  Business letter, 64–65
  Chester, 149
  Collecting, 5
  Colorful vocabulary, 105
  Combining sentences, 91
  Comparison and contrast, 71
  Complements to rubrics, 5
  Complex sentences, 87
  Confidential Key, 10, 74, 76
  Correct Use of the Apostrophe, 145
  Creak-Bang-Thud, 49

Developing instructional resources from, 13
Dictation, 147
Disappointment, 22
Distracting sentences, 37, 38
Expanding role of, 5–13
First-person writing, 133
Fluff My Cat, 57, 58
Forever Mine, 111, 112
Gathering, 13
Ghosts, 111, 112
Grade-level, 9, 12
Hockey Future, 16, 18
How the Pros Do It, 27, 28, 29
How the Raccoon Got Its Mask, 82, 83
Identifying personally effective writing strategies, 20
Instructional resource, 5–9
Intensifying voice, 136, 137
Keeping Out the Mongols, 101–2
Larry's Surprise, 123, 124
Learning about effective writing, 6
Learning from work with, 9–11
Learning sequence for work with writing, 8
Life on Earth in 2005, 92, 93
Lost Surfers, 149
Making a Difference, 78
My Father's Old Sweater, 128, 129
Mysterious Box, 10, 89, 113, 114, 115, 116
Ol' Freddy, 42
Openings, 51
Original imagery, 131
Painful Freedoms, 53–54
Planning strategies, 34–35
Playful activities, 59–60, 80–81, 98–99, 125–26
Poems, 129
Principles for collecting, 12
Reconsidering Interpretations, 30, 31, 32
Respect Police Officers, 75
Sentence Structure and Word Choice, 12
Showing, Not Telling, 22, 56
Smarty Pants and the Biggest Discovery, 16, 19
Student, 9, 13
The Bird and the Dog, 47
The House on the Hill, 66, 67
The Mirror of Vanity, 57, 58
The Perfect Pet, 138, 139
The Sandpit Setback, 107, 108
The Undefeatable Penguin, 40
The Year 2005, 73
Understanding Myself as a Writer, 21
Varied sentence types, 95

Verbs, 143
Vocabulary, 110
Volley, 96
What Is Normal, Anyway?, 69
Expository texts, 68
    Openings, 50–51, 52
    Pre-writing, 68, 150

Figures of speech, 130, 134
First-person writing, 132
Focused goal setting, 14, 24–26

Gifted writers, 138
Goal setting, 20, 24
    Focused, 14, 24–26

How the pros do it, 14, 27–29, 152

Identifying specific strategies, 14, 20–21
Informational text, 11
    Relevant and irrelevant detail, 37–38

Metaphors, 130
Myths, 82

Narrative texts, 11, 77
    Planning strategy, 66
    Relevant and irrelevant detail, 39–40
    Strong endings for, 48–49

Organization, 6, 7, 15, 16, 61–83
    Paragraph play, 61, 80–81
    Paragraphing with pizzazz, 61, 72–73
    Planning a myth, 61, 82–83
    Pre-writing for business letters, 61, 62–65
    Pre-writing for comparison and contrast, 61, 70–71
    Pre-writing for exposition, 61, 68–69
    Somebody, wanted, but, so, then, 61, 66–67
    Terrific transition, 61, 74–76
    Text sequencing to learn about transition, 61, 77–79
Original imagery, 130

Paragraphs, 72, 80
    Concluding, 62
    Introductory, 62
    Middle, 62
    Movement, 80
Participial phrase, 85, 88
Participle, 85

Parts of speech, 141
Permission form, 12
Personal writing goals, 24
Pre-writing exercises, 134
    Comparison and contrast, 70
    Exposition, 68
Prepositional phrase, 85, 88
Privacy laws, 12
Prose Models approach, 9
Purpose, 15, 36

RAFTS, 20, 33, 41
Reconsidering interpretations, 14, 30–32, 153
Relevant and irrelevant detail
    Informational text, 37–38
    Narrative text, 39–40
Revising with specific criteria, 14, 22–23
Revision, 22, 72, 115, 148
Rubrics
    Assessing student writing, 5, 115
    Traits of good writing, 6, 7, 13

Self-assessment of writing, 17, 151
Sentence structure/variety, 6, 7, 15, 16, 84–102
    Complex sentences, 84, 85–87
    Power of short sentences, 84, 96–97
    Sentence combining for interest and clarity, 84, 88–89
    Sentence combining to show relationships, 84, 90–91
    Sentence structure and word choice, 84, 100–102
    Simplifying the complex, 84, 98–99
    Varied sentence beginnings, 84, 92–93
    Varied sentence types, 84, 94–95
Sentences
    Beginnings, 92
    Combining, 88, 90
    Complex, 8, 85–86, 88, 90, 96, 98
    Compound, 85, 86, 90
    Declarative, 94
    Distracting, 37
    Effective, 138
    Exclamatory, 94
    Imperative, 94
    Interrogative, 94
    Off-topic insertions, 59
    Periodic, 86
    Short, 15, 96, 132
    Simple, 8, 85, 90, 98
    Topic, 52, 70, 72

Varied types, 94
Similes, 33, 130
Somebody, wanted, but, so, then, 33, 39, 66
Sticky notes, 10, 17, 22, 94, 109, 138, 148
Story beginnings, 43
    Expository, 50–51, 68
    Sentences, 92
Story endings, 10, 45, 48
    Expository, 68
    Strong, 48–49
Strategies
    After drafting, 20
    Before drafting, 20
    During drafting, 20
    Effective planning strategies, 14, 33–35
    Focused goal setting, 14, 20, 24–26
    How the pros do it, 14, 27–29
    Identifying specific strategies, 14, 20–21
    Reconsidering interpretations, 14, 30–32
    Revising with specific criteria, 14, 22–23
    Thinking about strong writing, 14, 15–19
Subordinate clause, 85, 88
Synonyms, 109

Text sequencing, 77, 79
Thing alternatives, 109
Thinking about strong writing, 14, 15–19
Titles, 57
Topic sentences, 72
    Effective and ineffective, 52–54
Transition, 12, 74, 77, 80, 92
    Examples of expressions, 74
    Text sequencing to learn about, 77, 79

Usage, 144, 146

Venn diagram, 70
Verbs, 111, 141, 143
    Challenge, 113
    Colorful, 117, 119
    Exemplars, 143
Vocabulary
    Assessing, 119
    Choices, 104, 106
    Connotative, 104, 109, 125
Voice, 6, 7, 15, 16, 127–39
    Active, 117
    Characteristics, 128
    First-person writing and dialogue, 127, 132–33
    Honest, original expression, 127, 128–29

Imaginative detail and use of devices, 127, 138–39
Intensifying, 127, 134–37
Original imagery, 127, 130–31
Passive, 117
Unique, 12

Word choice, 6, 7, 12, 15, 16, 103–26
Adding rich details, 103, 119–121
Assessing, 103, 115–16
Choices in context, 103, 122–24
Cloze for colorful vocabulary, 103, 104–5
Colorful choices, 103, 111–12
Effective, 10, 119
From descriptive to dull, 103, 125–26
Precise and imprecise, 103, 106–8
Rubric for scoring, 120
Sentence structure, 100
To be or not to be, 103, 117–18

Verb challenge, 103, 113–14
Vocabulary thing, 103, 109–10
Writing
Characteristics, 15
Cooperative, 80
Effective, 6, 7, 9, 13, 15, 36
Expository, 33, 50–51, 52, 68
First-person, 132
Good, 15
Informational, 11, 37–38, 70
Memorable, 55
Narrative, 11, 39–40, 48–49, 66, 77
RAFTS, 20, 33, 41
Self-assessment, 17, 151
Setting goals to improve, 17
Strong, 15–16
Weak, 16

Acknowledgments

The authors gratefully acknowledge Dr. Jean Hoeft of the Calgary Regional Professional Development Consortium for sponsoring a workshop sequence on the use of exemplars to teach writing. The following project participants contributed some of the exemplars and learning activities included in this book: Shirley Coughlan, Karen Dahlgren, Jen Deyenberg, Eric Dyck, Kerry Fleming, Ashley Gaston, Jennifer Harriman, Ingrid Harrison, Jenn Hohenstein, Carrie Hughes-McGuinness, Tammy Kolody, Erin Kurt, Pauline Miller, Scott Newman, Linda Nikolaj, Taira Prosk, and Jennifer Williams.

In addition, the authors thank the teachers at Clear Water Academy in Calgary, Alberta, for collecting and submitting the student work featured in this book.